THE ADVENTURES OF HUCKLEBERRY FINN

Mark Twain

SPARK PUBLISHING

122 Fifth Avenue
New York, NY 10011
www.sparknotes.com

ISBN 978-1-4114-6939-6

Please submit changes or report errors to www.sparknotes.com/errors.

Printed in Canada

10

Contents

CONTEXT   1

PLOT OVERVIEW   4

CHARACTER LIST   7

ANALYSIS OF MAJOR CHARACTERS   10
   HUCK FINN   10
   JIM   11
   TOM SAWYER   11

THEMES, MOTIFS & SYMBOLS   13
   RACISM AND SLAVERY   13
   INTELLECTUAL AND MORAL EDUCATION   14
   THE HYPOCRISY OF "CIVILIZED" SOCIETY   14
   CHILDHOOD   15
   LIES AND CONS   15
   SUPERSTITIONS AND FOLK BELIEFS   16
   PARODIES OF POPULAR ROMANCE NOVELS   16
   THE MISSISSIPPI RIVER   17

SUMMARY & ANALYSIS   18
   NOTICE AND EXPLANATORY   18
   CHAPTER I   19
   CHAPTERS II–III   22
   CHAPTERS IV–VI   25
   CHAPTERS VII–X   27
   CHAPTERS XI–XIII   30
   CHAPTERS XIV–XVI   33
   CHAPTERS XVII–XIX   35
   CHAPTERS XX–XXII   39
   CHAPTERS XXIII–XXV   41
   CHAPTERS XXVI–XXVIII   44
   CHAPTERS XXIX–XXXI   47
   CHAPTERS XXXII–XXXV   49
   CHAPTERS XXXVI–XXXIX   52
   CHAPTERS XL–XLIII   54

IMPORTANT QUOTATIONS EXPLAINED   58

KEY FACTS   63

STUDY QUESTIONS   66

HOW TO WRITE LITERARY ANALYSIS   68
    THE LITERARY ESSAY: A STEP-BY-STEP GUIDE   68
    SUGGESTED ESSAY TOPICS   80
    A+ STUDENT ESSAY   81
    GLOSSARY OF LITERARY TERMS   83
    A NOTE ON PLAGIARISM   85

REVIEW & RESOURCES   86
    QUIZ   86
    SUGGESTIONS FOR FURTHER READING   92

CONTEXT

MARK TWAIN WAS born Samuel Langhorne Clemens in the town of Florida, Missouri, in 1835. When he was four years old, his family moved to Hannibal, a town on the Mississippi River much like the towns depicted in his two most famous novels, *The Adventures of Tom Sawyer* (1876) and *The Adventures of Huckleberry Finn (1884)*.

Clemens spent his young life in a fairly affluent family that owned a number of household slaves. The death of Clemens's father in 1847, however, left the family in hardship. Clemens left school, worked for a printer, and, in 1851, having finished his apprenticeship, began to set type for his brother Orion's newspaper, the *Hannibal Journal*. But Hannibal proved too small to hold Clemens, who soon became a sort of itinerant printer and found work in a number of American cities, including New York and Philadelphia.

While still in his early twenties, Clemens gave up his printing career in order to work on riverboats on the Mississippi. Clemens eventually became a riverboat pilot, and his life on the river influenced him a great deal. Perhaps most important, the riverboat life provided him with the pen name Mark Twain, derived from the riverboat leadsmen's signal—"By the mark, twain"—that the water was deep enough for safe passage. Life on the river also gave Twain material for several of his books, including the raft scenes of *Huckleberry Finn* and the material for his autobiographical *Life on the Mississippi (1883)*.

Clemens continued to work on the river until 1861, when the Civil War exploded across America and shut down the Mississippi for travel and shipping. Although Clemens joined a Confederate cavalry division, he was no ardent Confederate, and when his division deserted en masse, he did too. He then made his way west with his brother Orion, working first as a silver miner in Nevada and then stumbling into his true calling, journalism. In 1863, Clemens began to sign articles with the name Mark Twain.

Throughout the late 1860s and 1870s, Twain's articles, stories, memoirs, and novels, characterized by an irrepressible wit and a deft ear for language and dialect, garnered him immense celebrity. His novel *The Innocents Abroad* (1869) was an instant bestseller, and *The Adventures of Tom Sawyer* (1876) received even greater national acclaim and cemented Twain's position as a giant in American literary circles. As the nation prospered economically in the post–Civil War period—an era that came to be known as the Gilded Age, an epithet that Twain coined—so too did Twain. His books were sold door-to-door, and he became wealthy enough to build a large house in Hartford, Connecticut, for himself and his wife, Olivia, whom he had married in 1870.

Twain began work on *Huckleberry Finn*, a sequel to *Tom Sawyer*, in an effort to capitalize on the popularity of the earlier novel. This new novel took on a more serious character, however, as Twain focused increasingly on the institution of slavery and the South. Twain soon set *Huckleberry Finn* aside, perhaps because its darker tone did not fit the optimistic sentiments of the Gilded Age. In the early 1880s, however, the hopefulness of the post–Civil War years began to fade. Reconstruction, the political program designed to reintegrate the defeated South into the Union as a slavery-free region, began to fail. The harsh measures the victorious North imposed only embittered the South. Concerned about maintaining power, many Southern politicians began an effort to control and oppress the black men and women whom the war had freed.

Meanwhile, Twain's personal life began to collapse. His wife had long been sickly, and the couple lost their first son after just nineteen months. Twain also made a number of poor investments and financial decisions and, in 1891, found himself mired in debilitating debt. As his personal fortune dwindled, he continued to devote himself to writing. Drawing from his personal plight and the prevalent national troubles of the day, he finished a draft of *Huckleberry Finn* in 1883, and by 1884 had it ready for publication. The novel met with great public and critical acclaim.

Twain continued to write over the next ten years. He published two more popular novels, *A Connecticut Yankee in King Arthur's Court* (1889) and *Pudd'nhead Wilson* (1894), but went into a considerable decline afterward, never again publishing work that matched the high standard he had set with *Huckleberry Finn*. Personal tragedy also continued to hound Twain: his finances remained troublesome, and within the course of a few years, his wife and two of his daughters passed away. Twain's writing from this period until the end of his life reflects a depression and a sort of righteous rage at the injustices of the world. Despite his personal troubles, however,

Twain continued to enjoy immense esteem and fame and continued to be in demand as a public speaker until his death in 1910.

The story of *Huckleberry Finn*, however, does not end with the death of its author. Through the twentieth century, the novel has become famous not merely as the crown jewel in the work of one of America's preeminent writers, but also as a subject of intense controversy. The novel occasionally has been banned in Southern states because of its steadfastly critical take on the South and the hypocrisies of slavery. Others have dismissed *Huckleberry Finn* as vulgar or racist because it uses the word *nigger,* a term whose connotations obscure the novel's deeper themes—which are unequivocally antislavery—and even prevent some from reading and enjoying it altogether. The fact that the historical context in which Twain wrote made his use of the word insignificant—and, indeed, part of the realism he wanted to create—offers little solace to some modern readers. Ultimately, *The Adventures of Huckleberry Finn* has proved significant not only as a novel that explores the racial and moral world of its time but also, through the controversies that continue to surround it, as an artifact of those same moral and racial tensions as they have evolved to the present day.

Plot Overview

THE ADVENTURES OF HUCKLEBERRY FINN opens by familiarizing us with the events of the novel that preceded it, *The Adventures of Tom Sawyer*. Both novels are set in the town of St. Petersburg, Missouri, which lies on the banks of the Mississippi River. At the end of *Tom Sawyer*, Huckleberry Finn, a poor boy with a drunken bum for a father, and his friend Tom Sawyer, a middle-class boy with an imagination too active for his own good, found a robber's stash of gold. As a result of his adventure, Huck gained quite a bit of money, which the bank held for him in trust. Huck was adopted by the Widow Douglas, a kind but stifling woman who lives with her sister, the self-righteous Miss Watson.

As *Huckleberry Finn* opens, Huck is none too thrilled with his new life of cleanliness, manners, church, and school. However, he sticks it out at the bequest of Tom Sawyer, who tells him that in order to take part in Tom's new "robbers' gang," Huck must stay "respectable." All is well and good until Huck's brutish, drunken father, Pap, reappears in town and demands Huck's money. The local judge, Judge Thatcher, and the Widow try to get legal custody of Huck, but another well-intentioned new judge in town believes in the rights of Huck's natural father and even takes the old drunk into his own home in an attempt to reform him. This effort fails miserably, and Pap soon returns to his old ways. He hangs around town for several months, harassing his son, who in the meantime has learned to read and to tolerate the Widow's attempts to improve him. Finally, outraged when the Widow Douglas warns him to stay away from her house, Pap kidnaps Huck and holds him in a cabin across the river from St. Petersburg.

Whenever Pap goes out, he locks Huck in the cabin, and when he returns home drunk, he beats the boy. Tired of his confinement and fearing the beatings will worsen, Huck escapes from Pap by faking his own death, killing a pig and spreading its blood all over the cabin. Hiding on Jackson's Island in the middle of the Mississippi River, Huck watches the townspeople search the river for his body. After a few days on the island, he encounters Jim, one of Miss Watson's slaves. Jim has run away from Miss Watson after hearing her talk about selling him to a plantation down the river, where he would be treated horribly and separated from his wife and children.

Huck and Jim team up, despite Huck's uncertainty about the legality or morality of helping a runaway slave. While they camp out on the island, a great storm causes the Mississippi to flood. Huck and Jim spy a log raft and a house floating past the island. They capture the raft and loot the house, finding in it the body of a man who has been shot. Jim refuses to let Huck see the dead man's face.

Although the island is blissful, Huck and Jim are forced to leave after Huck learns from a woman onshore that her husband has seen smoke coming from the island and believes that Jim is hiding out there. Huck also learns that a reward has been offered for Jim's capture. Huck and Jim start downriver on the raft, intending to leave it at the mouth of the Ohio River and proceed up that river by steamboat to the free states, where slavery is prohibited. Several days' travel takes them past St. Louis, and they have a close encounter with a gang of robbers on a wrecked steamboat. They manage to escape with the robbers' loot.

During a night of thick fog, Huck and Jim miss the mouth of the Ohio and encounter a group of men looking for escaped slaves. Huck has a brief moral crisis about concealing stolen "property"— Jim, after all, belongs to Miss Watson—but then lies to the men and tells them that his father is on the raft suffering from smallpox. Terrified of the disease, the men give Huck money and hurry away. Unable to backtrack to the mouth of the Ohio, Huck and Jim continue downriver. The next night, a steamboat slams into their raft, and Huck and Jim are separated.

Huck ends up in the home of the kindly Grangerfords, a family of Southern aristocrats locked in a bitter and silly feud with a neighboring clan, the Shepherdsons. The elopement of a Grangerford daughter with a Shepherdson son leads to a gun battle in which many in the families are killed. While Huck is caught up in the feud, Jim shows up with the repaired raft. Huck hurries to Jim's hiding place, and they take off down the river.

A few days later, Huck and Jim rescue a pair of men who are being pursued by armed bandits. The men, clearly con artists, claim to be a displaced English duke (the duke) and the long-lost heir to the French throne (the dauphin). Powerless to tell two white adults to leave, Huck and Jim continue down the river with the pair of "aristocrats." The duke and the dauphin pull several scams in the small towns along the river. Coming into one town, they hear the story of a man, Peter Wilks, who has recently died and left much of his inheritance to his two brothers, who should be arriving from England any day. The duke and the dauphin enter the town pretending to be Wilks's brothers. Wilks's three nieces welcome the con men and quickly set about liquidating the estate. A few townspeople become skeptical, and Huck, who grows to admire the Wilks sisters, decides to thwart the scam. He steals the dead Peter Wilks's gold from the duke and the dauphin but is forced to stash it in Wilks's coffin. Huck then reveals all to the eldest Wilks sister, Mary Jane. Huck's plan for exposing the duke and the dauphin is about to unfold when Wilks's real brothers arrive from England. The angry townspeople hold both sets of Wilks claimants, and the duke and the dauphin just barely escape in the ensuing confusion. Fortunately for the sisters, the gold is found. Unfortunately for Huck and Jim, the duke and the dauphin make it back to the raft just as Huck and Jim are pushing off.

After a few more small scams, the duke and dauphin commit their worst crime yet: they sell Jim to a local farmer, telling him Jim is a runaway for whom a large reward is being offered. Huck finds out where Jim is being held and resolves to free him. At the house where Jim is a prisoner, a woman greets Huck excitedly and calls him "Tom." As Huck quickly discovers, the people holding Jim are none other than Tom Sawyer's aunt and uncle, Silas and Sally Phelps. The Phelpses mistake Huck for Tom, who is due to arrive for a visit, and Huck goes along with their mistake. He intercepts Tom between the Phelps house and the steamboat dock, and Tom pretends to be his own younger brother, Sid.

Tom hatches a wild plan to free Jim, adding all sorts of unnecessary obstacles even though Jim is only lightly secured. Huck is sure Tom's plan will get them all killed, but he complies nonetheless. After a seeming eternity of pointless preparation, during which the boys ransack the Phelps's house and make Aunt Sally miserable, they put the plan into action. Jim is freed, but a pursuer shoots Tom in the leg. Huck is forced to get a doctor, and Jim sacrifices his freedom to nurse Tom. All are returned to the Phelps's house, where Jim ends up back in chains.

When Tom wakes the next morning, he reveals that Jim has actually been a free man all along, as Miss Watson, who made a provision in her will to free Jim, died two months earlier. Tom had planned the entire escape idea all as a game and had intended to pay Jim for his troubles. Tom's Aunt Polly then shows up, identifying "Tom" and "Sid" as Huck and Tom. Jim tells Huck, who fears for his future—particularly that his father might reappear—that the body they found on the floating house off Jackson's Island had been Pap's. Aunt Sally then steps in and offers to adopt Huck, but Huck, who has had enough "sivilizing," announces his plan to set out for the West.

CHARACTER LIST

Huckleberry Finn The protagonist and narrator of the novel.
Huck is the thirteen-year-old son of the local drunk
of St. Petersburg, Missouri, a town on the Mississippi
River. Frequently forced to survive on his own wits
and always a bit of an outcast, Huck is thoughtful,
intelligent (though formally uneducated), and willing
to come to his own conclusions about important
matters, even if these conclusions contradict society's
norms. Nevertheless, Huck is still a boy, and is
influenced by others, particularly by his imaginative
friend, Tom.

Tom Sawyer Huck's friend, and the protagonist of *Tom Sawyer,*
the novel to which *Huckleberry Finn* is ostensibly
the sequel. In *Huckleberry Finn,* Tom serves as a foil
to Huck: imaginative, dominating, and given to wild
plans taken from the plots of adventure novels, Tom is
everything that Huck is not. Tom's stubborn reliance
on the "authorities" of romance novels leads him to
acts of incredible stupidity and startling cruelty. His
rigid adherence to society's conventions aligns Tom
with the "sivilizing" forces that Huck learns to see
through and gradually abandons.

Widow Douglas and Miss Watson Two wealthy sisters who live
together in a large house in St. Petersburg and who
adopt Huck. The gaunt and severe Miss Watson is
the most prominent representative of the hypocritical
religious and ethical values Twain criticizes in the
novel. The Widow Douglas is somewhat gentler in her
beliefs and has more patience with the mischievous
Huck. When Huck acts in a manner contrary to
societal expectations, it is the Widow Douglas whom
he fears disappointing.

Jim One of Miss Watson's household slaves. Jim is
superstitious and occasionally sentimental, but he is

also intelligent, practical, and ultimately more of an adult than anyone else in the novel. Jim's frequent acts of selflessness, his longing for his family, and his friendship with both Huck and Tom demonstrate to Huck that humanity has nothing to do with race. Because Jim is a black man and a runaway slave, he is at the mercy of almost all the other characters in the novel and is often forced into ridiculous and degrading situations.

Pap   Huck's father, the town drunk and ne'er-do-well. Pap is a wreck when he appears at the beginning of the novel, with disgusting, ghostlike white skin and tattered clothes. The illiterate Pap disapproves of Huck's education and beats him frequently. Pap represents both the general debasement of white society and the failure of family structures in the novel.

The duke and the dauphin   A pair of con men whom Huck and Jim rescue as they are being run out of a river town. The older man, who appears to be about seventy, claims to be the "dauphin," the son of King Louis XVI and heir to the French throne. The younger man, who is about thirty, claims to be the usurped Duke of Bridgewater. Although Huck quickly realizes the men are frauds, he and Jim remain at their mercy, as Huck is only a child and Jim is a runaway slave. The duke and the dauphin carry out a number of increasingly disturbing swindles as they travel down the river on the raft.

Judge Thatcher   The local judge who shares responsibility for Huck with the Widow Douglas and is in charge of safeguarding the money that Huck and Tom found at the end of *Tom Sawyer*. When Huck discovers that Pap has returned to town, he wisely signs his fortune over to the Judge, who doesn't really accept the money, but tries to comfort Huck. Judge Thatcher has a daughter, Becky, who was Tom's girlfriend in *Tom Sawyer* and whom Huck calls "Bessie" in this novel.

The Grangerfords A family that takes Huck in after a steamboat hits his raft, separating him from Jim. The kindhearted Grangerfords, who offer Huck a place to stay in their tacky country home, are locked in a long-standing feud with another local family, the Shepherdsons. Twain uses the two families to engage in some rollicking humor and to mock a overly romanticizes ideas about family honor. Ultimately, the families' sensationalized feud gets many of them killed.

The Wilks family At one point during their travels, the duke and the dauphin encounter a man who tells them of the death of a local named Peter Wilks, who has left behind a rich estate. The man inadvertently gives the con men enough information to allow them to pretend to be Wilks's two brothers from England, who are the recipients of much of the inheritance. The duke and the dauphin's subsequent conning of the good-hearted and vulnerable Wilks sisters is the first step in the con men's increasingly cruel series of scams, which culminate in the sale of Jim.

Silas and Sally Phelps Tom Sawyer's aunt and uncle, whom Huck coincidentally encounters in his search for Jim after the con men have sold him. Sally is the sister of Tom's aunt, Polly. Essentially good people, the Phelpses nevertheless hold Jim in custody and try to return him to his rightful owner. Silas and Sally are the unknowing victims of many of Tom and Huck's "preparations" as they try to free Jim. The Phelpses are the only intact and functional family in this novel, yet they are too much for Huck, who longs to escape their "sivilizing" influence.

Aunt Polly Tom Sawyer's aunt and guardian and Sally Phelps's sister. Aunt Polly appears at the end of the novel and properly identifies Huck, who has pretended to be Tom, and Tom, who has pretended to be his own younger brother, Sid.

CHARACTER LIST

ANALYSIS OF MAJOR CHARACTERS

HUCK FINN

From the beginning of the novel, Twain makes it clear that Huck is a boy who comes from the lowest levels of white society. His father is a drunk and a ruffian who disappears for months on end. Huck himself is dirty and frequently homeless. Although the Widow Douglas attempts to "reform" Huck, he resists her attempts and maintains his independent ways. The community has failed to protect him from his father, and though the Widow finally gives Huck some of the schooling and religious training that he had missed, he has not been indoctrinated with social values in the same way a middle-class boy like Tom Sawyer has been. Huck's distance from mainstream society makes him skeptical of the world around him and the ideas it passes on to him.

Huck's instinctual distrust and his experiences as he travels down the river force him to question the things society has taught him. According to the law, Jim is Miss Watson's property, but according to Huck's sense of logic and fairness, it seems "right" to help Jim. Huck's natural intelligence and his willingness to think through a situation on its own merits lead him to some conclusions that are correct in their context but that would shock white society. For example, Huck discovers, when he and Jim meet a group of slave-hunters, that telling a lie is sometimes the right course of action.

Because Huck is a child, the world seems new to him. Everything he encounters is an occasion for thought. Because of his background, however, he does more than just apply the rules that he has been taught—he creates his own rules. Yet Huck is not some kind of independent moral genius. He must still struggle with some of the preconceptions about blacks that society has ingrained in him, and at the end of the novel, he shows himself all too willing to follow Tom Sawyer's lead. But even these failures are part of what makes Huck appealing and sympathetic. He is only a boy, after all, and therefore fallible. Imperfect as he is, Huck represents what anyone is capable of becoming: a thinking, feeling human being rather than a mere cog in the machine of society.

JIM

Jim, Huck's companion as he travels down the river, is a man of remarkable intelligence and compassion. At first glance, Jim seems to be superstitious to the point of idiocy, but a careful reading of the time that Huck and Jim spend on Jackson's Island reveals that Jim's superstitions conceal a deep knowledge of the natural world and represent an alternate form of "truth" or intelligence. Moreover, Jim has one of the few healthy, functioning families in the novel. Although he has been separated from his wife and children, he misses them terribly, and it is only the thought of a permanent separation from them that motivates his criminal act of running away from Miss Watson. On the river, Jim becomes a surrogate father, as well as a friend, to Huck, taking care of him without being intrusive or smothering. He cooks for the boy and shelters him from some of the worst horrors that they encounter, including the sight of Pap's corpse, and, for a time, the news of his father's passing.

Some readers have criticized Jim as being too passive, but it is important to remember that he remains at the mercy of every other character in this novel, including even the poor, thirteen-year-old Huck, as the letter that Huck nearly sends to Miss Watson demonstrates. Like Huck, Jim is realistic about his situation and must find ways of accomplishing his goals without incurring the wrath of those who could turn him in. In this position, he is seldom able to act boldly or speak his mind. Nonetheless, despite these restrictions and constant fear, Jim consistently acts as a noble human being and a loyal friend. In fact, Jim could be described as the only real adult in the novel, and the only one who provides a positive, respectable example for Huck to follow.

TOM SAWYER

Tom is the same age as Huck and his best friend. Whereas Huck's birth and upbringing have left him in poverty and on the margins of society, Tom has been raised in relative comfort. As a result, his beliefs are an unfortunate combination of what he has learned from the adults around him and the fanciful notions he has gleaned from reading romance and adventure novels. Tom believes in sticking strictly to "rules," most of which have more to do with style than with morality or anyone's welfare. Tom is thus the perfect foil for Huck: his rigid adherence to rules and precepts contrasts with Huck's tendency to question authority and think for himself.

Although Tom's escapades are often funny, they also show just how disturbingly and unthinkingly cruel society can be. Tom knows all along that Miss Watson has died and that Jim is now a free man, yet he is willing to allow Jim to remain a captive while he entertains himself with fantastic escape plans. Tom's plotting tortures not only Jim, but Aunt Sally and Uncle Silas as well. In the end, although he is just a boy like Huck and is appealing in his zest for adventure and his unconscious wittiness, Tom embodies what a young, well-to-do white man is raised to become in the society of his time: self-centered with dominion over all.

THEMES, MOTIFS & SYMBOLS

THEMES

Themes are the fundamental and often universal ideas explored in a literary work.

RACISM AND SLAVERY

Although Twain wrote *Huckleberry Finn* two decades after the Emancipation Proclamation and the end of the Civil War, America—and especially the South—was still struggling with racism and the aftereffects of slavery. By the early 1880s, Reconstruction, the plan to put the United States back together after the war and integrate freed slaves into society, had hit shaky ground, although it had not yet failed outright. As Twain worked on his novel, race relations, which seemed to be on a positive path in the years following the Civil War, once again became strained. The imposition of Jim Crow laws, designed to limit the power of blacks in the South in a variety of indirect ways, brought the beginning of a new, insidious effort to oppress. The new racism of the South, less institutionalized and monolithic, was also more difficult to combat. Slavery could be outlawed, but when white Southerners enacted racist laws or policies under a professed motive of self-defense against newly freed blacks, far fewer people, Northern or Southern, saw the act as immoral and rushed to combat it.

Although Twain wrote the novel after slavery was abolished, he set it several decades earlier, when slavery was still a fact of life. But even by Twain's time, things had not necessarily gotten much better for blacks in the South. In this light, we might read Twain's depiction of slavery as an allegorical representation of the condition of blacks in the United States even *after* the abolition of slavery. Just as slavery places the noble and moral Jim under the control of white society, no matter how degraded that white society may be, so too did the insidious racism that arose near the end of Reconstruction oppress black men for illogical and hypocritical reasons. In *Huckleberry Finn*, Twain, by exposing the hypocrisy of slavery, demonstrates how racism distorts the oppressors as much as it does those who are oppressed. The result is a world of moral confusion, in which seemingly "good" white people such as Miss Watson and Sally Phelps express no concern about the injustice of slavery or the cruelty of separating Jim from his family.

INTELLECTUAL AND MORAL EDUCATION

By focusing on Huck's education, *Huckleberry Finn* fits into the tradition of the bildungsroman: a novel depicting an individual's maturation and development. As a poor, uneducated boy, for all intents and purposes an orphan, Huck distrusts the morals and precepts of the society that treats him as an outcast and fails to protect him from abuse. This apprehension about society, and his growing relationship with Jim, lead Huck to question many of the teachings that he has received, especially regarding race and slavery. More than once, we see Huck choose to "go to hell" rather than go along with the rules and follow what he has been taught. Huck bases these decisions on his experiences, his own sense of logic, and what his developing conscience tells him. On the raft, away from civilization, Huck is especially free from society's rules, able to make his own decisions without restriction. Through deep introspection, he comes to his own conclusions, unaffected by the accepted—and often hypocritical—rules and values of Southern culture. By the novel's end, Huck has learned to "read" the world around him, to distinguish good, bad, right, wrong, menace, friend, and so on. His moral development is sharply contrasted to the character of Tom Sawyer, who is influenced by a bizarre mix of adventure novels and Sunday-school teachings, which he combines to justify his outrageous and potentially harmful escapades.

THE HYPOCRISY OF "CIVILIZED" SOCIETY

When Huck plans to head west at the end of the novel in order to escape further "sivilizing," he is trying to avoid more than regular baths and mandatory school attendance. Throughout the novel, Twain depicts the society that surrounds Huck as little more than a collection of degraded rules and precepts that defy logic. This faulty logic appears early in the novel, when the new judge in town allows Pap to keep custody of Huck. The judge privileges Pap's "rights" to his son as his natural father over Huck's welfare. At the same time, this decision comments on a system that puts a white man's rights to his "property"—his slaves—over the welfare and freedom of a black man. In implicitly comparing the plight of slaves to the plight of Huck at the hands of Pap, Twain implies that it is impossible for a society that owns slaves to be just, no matter how "civilized" that society believes and proclaims itself to be. Again and again, Huck encounters individuals who seem good—Sally Phelps, for example—but who Twain takes care to show are prejudiced slave-owners. This shaky sense of justice that Huck repeatedly encounters lies at the heart of society's problems: terrible acts go unpunished, yet frivolous crimes, such as drunkenly shouting insults, lead to executions. Sherburn's speech to the mob that has come to lynch him accurately summarizes the view of society Twain gives in *Huckleberry Finn*: rather than maintain collective welfare, society instead is marked by cowardice, a lack of logic, and profound selfishness.

MOTIFS

Motifs are recurring structures, contrasts, and literary devices that can help to develop and inform the text's major themes.

CHILDHOOD

Huck's youth is an important factor in his moral education over the course of the novel, for we sense that only a child is open-minded enough to undergo the kind of development that Huck does. Since Huck and Tom are young, their age lends a sense of play to their actions, which excuses them in certain ways and also deepens the novel's commentary on slavery and society. Ironically, Huck often knows better than the adults around him, even though he has lacked the guidance that a proper family and community should have offered him. Twain also frequently draws links between Huck's youth and Jim's status as a black man: both are vulnerable, yet Huck, because he is white, has power over Jim. And on a different level, the silliness, pure joy, and naïveté of childhood give *Huckleberry Finn* a sense of fun and humor. Though its themes are quite weighty, the novel itself feels light in tone and is an enjoyable read because of this rambunctious childhood excitement that enlivens the story.

LIES AND CONS

Huckleberry Finn is full of malicious lies and scams, many of them coming from the duke and the dauphin. It is clear that these con men's lies are bad, for they hurt a number of innocent people. Yet Huck himself tells a number of lies and even cons a few people, most notably the slave-hunters, to whom he makes up a story about a smallpox outbreak in order to protect Jim. As Huck realizes, it seems that telling a lie can actually be a good thing, depending on its purpose. This insight is part of Huck's learning process, as he finds that some of the rules he has been taught contradict what seems to be "right." At other points, the lines between a con, legitimate entertainment, and approved social structures like religion are fine indeed. In this light, lies and cons provide an effective way for Twain to highlight the moral ambiguity that runs through the novel.

SUPERSTITIONS AND FOLK BELIEFS

From the time Huck meets him on Jackson's Island until the end of the novel, Jim spouts a wide range of superstitions and folktales. Whereas Jim initially appears foolish to believe so unwaveringly in these kinds of signs and omens, it turns out, curiously, that many of his beliefs do indeed have some basis in reality or presage events to come. Much as we do, Huck at first dismisses most of Jim's superstitions as silly, but ultimately he comes to appreciate Jim's deep knowledge of the world. In this sense, Jim's superstition serves as an alternative to accepted social teachings and assumptions and provides a reminder that mainstream conventions are not always right.

PARODIES OF POPULAR ROMANCE NOVELS

Huckleberry Finn is full of people who base their lives on romantic literary models and stereotypes of various kinds. Tom Sawyer, the most obvious example, bases his life and actions on adventure novels. The deceased Emmeline Grangerford painted weepy maidens and wrote poems about dead children in the romantic style. The Shepherdson and Grangerford families kill one another out of a bizarre, overexcited conception of family honor. These characters' proclivities toward the romantic allow Twain a few opportunities to indulge in some fun, and indeed, the episodes that deal with this subject are among the funniest in the novel. However, there is a more substantive message beneath: that popular literature is highly stylized and therefore rarely reflects the reality of a society. Twain shows how a strict adherence to these romantic ideals is ultimately dangerous: Tom is shot, Emmeline dies, and the Shepherdsons and Grangerfords end up in a deadly clash.

SYMBOLS

Symbols are objects, characters, figures, and colors used to represent abstract ideas or concepts.

THE MISSISSIPPI RIVER

For Huck and Jim, the Mississippi River is the ultimate symbol of freedom. Alone on their raft, they do not have to answer to anyone. The river carries them toward freedom: for Jim, toward the free states; for Huck, away from his abusive father and the restrictive "sivilizing" of St. Petersburg. Much like the river itself, Huck and Jim are in flux, willing to change their attitudes about each other with little prompting. Despite their freedom, however, they soon find that they are not completely free from the evils and influences of the towns on the river's banks. Even early on, the real world intrudes on the paradise of the raft: the river floods, bringing Huck and Jim into contact with criminals, wrecks, and stolen goods. Then, a thick fog causes them to miss the mouth of the Ohio River, which was to be their route to freedom.

As the novel progresses, then, the river becomes something other than the inherently benevolent place Huck originally thought it was. As Huck and Jim move further south, the duke and the dauphin invade the raft, and Huck and Jim must spend more time ashore. Though the river continues to offer a refuge from trouble, it often merely effects the exchange of one bad situation for another. Each escape exists in the larger context of a continual drift southward, toward the Deep South and entrenched slavery. In this transition from idyllic retreat to source of peril, the river mirrors the complicated state of the South. As Huck and Jim's journey progresses, the river, which once seemed a paradise and a source of freedom, becomes merely a short-term means of escape that nonetheless pushes Huck and Jim ever further toward danger and destruction.

SUMMARY & ANALYSIS

NOTICE AND EXPLANATORY

SUMMARY

The novel begins with a Notice from someone named G. G., who is identified as the Chief of Ordnance. The Notice demands that no one try to find a motive, moral, or plot in the novel, on pain of various and sundry punishments. The Notice is followed by an Explanatory note from the Author, which states that the attention to dialects in the book has been painstaking and is extremely true-to-life in mimicking the peculiar verbal tendencies of individuals along the Mississippi. It assures the reader that if he or she feels that the characters in the book are "trying to talk alike but failing," then the reader is mistaken.

ANALYSIS

The Notice and Explanatory set the tone for *The Adventures of Huckleberry Finn* through their mixing of humor and seriousness. In its declaration that anyone looking for motive, plot, or moral will be prosecuted, banished, or shot, the Notice establishes a sense of blustery comedy that pervades the rest of the novel. The Explanatory takes on a slightly different tone, still full of a general good-naturedness but also brimming with authority. In the final paragraph, Twain essentially dares the reader to believe that he might know or understand more about the dialects of the South, and, by extension, the South itself. Twain's good nature stems in part from his sense of assurance that, should anyone dare to challenge him, Twain would certainly prove victorious.

Beyond tone, the Notice and Explanatory set the stage for the themes that the novel explores later. Twain's coy statement about the lack of seriousness in *Huckleberry Finn* actually alerts us that such seriousness does in fact exist in the text. At the same time, Twain's refusal to make any straightforward claims for the seriousness of his work adds a note of irony and charm. The Explanatory note from the Author concerns the use of dialect, which Twain says has been reconstructed "painstakingly." Again, if *Huckleberry Finn* is not meant to be a "serious" novel, the claim seems strange. But it is a serious novel, and Twain's note on dialogue speaks for the authority and experience of the author and establishes the novel's antiromantic, realistic stance. In short, the Notice and Explanatory, which at first glance appear to be disposable jokes, link the novel's sense of fun and lightheartedness with its deeper moral concerns. This coupling continues throughout *Huckleberry Finn* and remains one of its greatest triumphs.

CHAPTER I

SUMMARY

> *. . . when I couldn't stand it no longer I lit out. I got into my old rags and my sugar-hogshead again, and was free and satisfied.* (See QUOTATIONS, *p. 58*)

The novel begins as the narrator (later identified as Huckleberry Finn) states that we may know of him from another book, *The Adventures of Tom Sawyer,* written by "Mr. Mark Twain." Huck quickly asserts that it "ain't no matter" if we haven't heard of him. According to Huck, Twain mostly told the truth in the previous tale, with some "stretchers" thrown in, although everyone—except Tom's Aunt Polly, the Widow Douglas, and maybe a few other girls—tells lies once in a while.

We learn that *Tom Sawyer* ended with Tom and Huckleberry finding a stash of gold some robbers had hidden in a cave. The boys received $6,000 apiece, which the local judge, Judge Thatcher, put into a trust. The money in the bank now accrues a dollar a day from interest. Then, the Widow Douglas adopted and tried to "sivilize" Huck. Huck couldn't stand it, so he threw on his old rags and ran away. He has since returned because Tom Sawyer told him he could join his new band of robbers if he would return to the Widow "and be respectable."

The Widow frequently bemoans her failure to reform Huck. He particularly cringes at the fact that he has to "grumble" (i.e., pray) over the food before every meal. The Widow tries to teach Huck about Moses, but Huck loses interest when he realizes that Moses is dead. The Widow will not let Huck smoke but approves of snuff since she uses it herself. Her sister, Miss Watson, tries to give Huck spelling lessons. These efforts are not in vain, as Huck does in fact learn to read.

Huck feels especially restless because the Widow and Miss Watson constantly attempt to improve his behavior. When Miss Watson tells him about the "bad place"—hell—he blurts out that he would like to go there, for a change of scenery. This proclamation causes an uproar. Huck doesn't see the point of going to the "good place" and resolves not to bother trying to get there. He keeps this sentiment a secret, however, because he doesn't want to cause more trouble. When Huck asks, Miss Watson tells him that there is no chance that Tom Sawyer will end up in heaven. Huck is glad "because I wanted him and me to be together."

One night, after Miss Watson leads a prayer session with Huck and the household slaves, Huck goes to bed feeling "so lonesome I most wished I was dead." He gets shivers hearing the sounds of nature through his window. Huck accidentally flicks a spider into a candle, and the bad omen frightens him. Just after midnight, Huck hears movement below the window and hears a "me-yow" sound, to which he responds with another "me-yow." Climbing out the window onto the shed, Huck finds Tom Sawyer waiting for him in the yard.

ANALYSIS

In the opening pages of *Huckleberry Finn,* we feel the presence of both Huck's narrative voice and Twain's voice as author. From the start, Huck speaks to us in a conversational tone that is very much his own but that also serves as a mouthpiece for Twain. When Huck mentions "Mr. Mark Twain" by name, he immediately gains an independence from his author: if he can mention his author, then in some sense he must exist on the same level that the author does. At the same time, Huck links Twain's new novel to *The Adventures of Tom Sawyer,* although he is careful to note that the two works are independent of one another and that we do not need to have read the previous novel to understand this one. Nevertheless, Twain does seek to take advantage of *Tom Sawyer*'s popularity by featuring the earlier novel's characters in this one.

Beyond establishing a voice, the first paragraph also conveys Huck's deeper personality. Huck is not just a poor boy with a humorous way of speaking and thinking; he is also a thoughtful young man who is willing and eager to question the "facts" of life and facets of human personality, such as the tendency to lie. The events in *Tom Sawyer* have already established Huck as a somewhat marginal character in the town of St. Petersburg. Although he is white, he is poor and therefore out of touch with civilized society. The novelty of practices like "grumbling" over food lends Huck's observations a humorous, fresh perspective on the foibles of society. Though Huck always remains open to learning, he never accepts new ideas without thinking, and he remains untainted by the rules and assumptions of the white society in which he finds himself. Though quick to comment on the absurdity of much of the world around him, Huck is not mean-spirited. He is equally quick to tell us that though the "widow cried over me, and called me a poor lost lamb . . . she never meant no harm by it."

The first chapter begins Twain's exploration of race and society, two of the major thematic concerns in *Huckleberry Finn*. We see quickly that, in the town of St. Petersburg, owning slaves is considered normal and unremarkable—even the Widow Douglas, a pious Christian, owns slaves. The slaves depicted in the novel are "household slaves," slaves who worked on small farms and in homes in which the master owned only a few slaves. Twain implicitly contrasts this type of slavery with the more brutal form of plantation slavery, in which hundreds of slaves worked for a single master, creating greater anonymity between slave and master, which in turn led to more backbreaking labor—and, often, extreme cruelty. Some critics have accused Twain of painting too soft a picture of slavery by not writing about plantation slaves. However, by depicting the "better" version of slavery, Twain is able to make a sharper criticism of the insidious dehumanization that accompanies *all* forms of slavery: the "lucky" household slaves, just like their counterparts on the plantations, are also in danger of having their families torn apart and are never considered fully human. Twain's portrayal suggests that if the "better" slavery is this terrible, the horrors of the "worse" type must be even more awful and dehumanizing. It is important to note here that Twain uses the word *nigger*, which has gotten *Huckleberry Finn* in trouble with many twentieth-century school boards, with a nonchalance that is certainly troubling to us today. The word would not have been disturbing in Twain's time, however, and is sadly necessary to any novel claiming to paint a realistic portrait of the slaveholding South at the time.

Twain's portrayal of slaveholding in this first chapter also raises questions about the hypocrisy and moral vacuity of society. Throughout the novel, Huck encounters seemingly good people who happen to own slaves—an incongruity that is never easily resolved. We are not meant to think that the Widow Douglas, for example, is thoroughly evil. People like the Widow serve as foils for Huck throughout the novel, as he tries to sort out the value of civilizing influences. Huck is a kind of natural philosopher, skeptical of social doctrines like religion and willing to set forth new ideas—for example, his idea that hell might actually be a better place than the Widow Douglas's heaven. Beneath the adventure story, *Huckleberry Finn* is a tale of Huck's moral development and of what his realizations can teach us about race, slavery, Southern society, and morality.

CHAPTERS II–III

SUMMARY & ANALYSIS

SUMMARY: CHAPTER II

Huck and Tom tiptoe through the Widow's garden. Huck trips on a root as he passes by the kitchen, and Jim, one of Miss Watson's slaves, hears him from inside. Tom and Huck crouch down and try to stay still, but Huck is struck by a series of uncontrollable itches, as often happens when he is in a situation "where it won't do for you to scratch." Jim says aloud that he will stay put until he discovers the source of the sound, but after several minutes, he falls asleep. Tom wants to tie Jim up, but the more practical Huck objects, so Tom settles for simply playing a trick by putting Jim's hat on a tree branch over Jim's head. Tom also takes candles from the kitchen, despite Huck's objections that they will risk getting caught.

Huck tells us that afterward, Jim tells everyone that some witches flew him around and put the hat atop his head. Jim expands the tale further, becoming a local celebrity among the slaves, who enjoy witch stories. Around his neck, Jim wears the five-cent piece Tom left for the candles, calling it a charm from the devil with the power to cure sickness. Huck notes somewhat sarcastically that Jim nearly becomes so "stuck up" from his newfound celebrity that he is unfit to be a servant.

Meanwhile, Tom and Huck meet up with a few other boys and take a boat to a large cave. There, Tom names his new band of robbers "Tom Sawyer's Gang." All must sign an oath in blood, vowing, among other things, to kill the family of any member who reveals the gang's secrets. The boys think it "a real beautiful oath," and Tom admits that he got part of it from books that he has read. The boys nearly disqualify Huck because he has no family aside from a drunken father who can never be found, but Huck appeases the boys by offering Miss Watson. Tom says the gang must capture and ransom people, although none of the boys knows what "ransom" means. Tom assumes it means to keep them captive until they die. In response to one boy's question, Tom tells the group that women are not to be killed but should be kept at the hideout, where the boys' manners will charm the women into falling in love with the boys. When one boy begins to cry out of homesickness and threatens to tell the group's secrets, Tom bribes him with five cents. They agree to meet again someday, but not on a Sunday, because that would be blasphemous. Huck makes it home and gets into bed just before dawn.

SUMMARY: CHAPTER III

After punishing Huck for dirtying his new clothes during his night out with Tom, Miss Watson tries to explain prayer to him. Huck gives up on it after some of his prayers are not answered. Miss Watson calls him a fool, and the Widow Douglas later explains that prayer bestows spiritual gifts, such as acting selflessly to help others. Huck, who cannot see any advantage in such gifts, resolves to forget the matter. The two women often take Huck aside for religious discussions, in which Widow Douglas describes a wonderful God, while Miss Watson describes a terrible one. Huck concludes there are two Gods and decides he would like to belong to Widow Douglas's, if He would take him. Huck considers this unlikely because of his bad qualities.

Meanwhile, a rumor circulates that Huck's Pap, who has not been seen in a year, is dead. A corpse was found in the river, thought to be Pap because of its "ragged" appearance. The face, however, was unrecognizable. At first, Huck is relieved. His father had been a drunk who beat him when he was sober, although Huck stayed hidden from him most of the time. Upon hearing further description of the body found, however, Huck realizes that it is not his father but rather a woman dressed in men's clothes. Huck worries that his father will soon reappear.

After a month in Tom's gang, Huck and the rest of the boys quit. With no actual robbing or killing going on, the gang's existence is pointless. Huck tells of one of Tom's more notable games, in which Tom pretended that a caravan of Arabs and Spaniards was going to camp nearby with hundreds of camels and elephants. It turned out to be a Sunday-school picnic, although Tom explained that it really was a caravan of Arabs and Spaniards—only they were enchanted, like in *Don Quixote*. The raid on the picnic netted the boys only a few doughnuts and jam but a fair amount of trouble. After testing another of Tom's theories by rubbing old lamps and rings but failing to summon a genie, Huck judges that most of Tom's stories have been "lies."

ANALYSIS: CHAPTERS II–III

These chapters establish Huck Finn and Tom Sawyer as foils for each other—characters whose actions and traits contrast each other in a way that gives us a better understanding of both of their characters. Twain uses Tom to satirize romantic literature and to comment on the darker side of so-called civilized society. Tom insists that his make-believe adventures be conducted "by the book." As Tom himself admits in regard to his gang's oath, he gets many of his ideas from fiction. In particular, Tom tries to emulate the romantic—that is, unrealistic, sensationalized, and sentimentalized—novels, mostly imported from Europe, that achieved enormous popularity in nineteenth-century America. Tom is identified with this romantic genre throughout the novel. Whereas Tom puts great stock in literary models, Huck is as skeptical of these as he is of religion. In both realms, Huck refuses to accept much on faith. He rejects both genies and prayers when they fail to produce the promised results. Twain makes this contrast between Tom's romanticism and Huck's skepticism to show that both points of view can prove equally misleading if taken to extremes.

Although Huck and Tom are set up as foils for one another, they still share some traits, which help to sustain their friendship throughout the novel. Perhaps most important, the two share a rambunctious boyishness; they delight in the dirty language and pranks that the adult world condemns. Yet Huck's feelings about society and the adult world are based on his negative experiences—most notably with his abusive father—and ring with a seriousness and weight that Tom's fancies lack. We get the sense that Tom can afford to accept the nonsense of society and romantic literature, but Huck cannot. On the whole, Huck's alienation from the "civilization" of the adult world is a bit starker and sadder.

Ironically, the novel that Tom explicitly mentions as a model for his actions is Cervantes's *Don Quixote*. In his masterpiece, Cervantes satirizes romantic adventure stories as Twain does in *Huckleberry Finn*. In referencing *Don Quixote,* Twain also gives a literary tip of the hat to one of the earliest and greatest picaresque novels, which, through its naïve protagonist's wacky adventures, satirizes literature, society, and human nature in much the same way that Twain does in *Huckleberry Finn*. By means of the reference to *Don Quixote,* Twain tells us that, though he intends to write a humorous novel, *Huckleberry Finn* also fits into a longstanding tradition of novels that seek to criticize through humor, to point out absurdity through absurdity. In this chapter, for instance, Twain comments on Tom's absurdity and blind ignorance in basing his actions on a novel that is so clearly a satire. Tom, who is interested in contracts, codes of conduct, fancy language, and make-believe ideas, believes in these frilly ideas at the expense of common sense. He cares more about absurd stylistic ideals than he does about people. Tom also displays some of the hypocrisy of civilized society. For instance, he makes the members of his gang sign an oath in blood and swear not to divulge the group's secrets, but when a boy threatens to betray that promise, Tom simply offers him a bribe.

CHAPTERS IV–VI

SUMMARY: CHAPTER IV
Over the next few months, Huck begins to adjust to his new life and even makes some progress in school. One winter morning, he notices boot tracks in the snow near the house. Within one heel print is the shape of two nails crossed to ward off the devil. Huck immediately recognizes this mark and runs to Judge Thatcher. Huck sells his fortune (the money he and Tom recovered in *Tom Sawyer*, which the Judge has been managing for him) to the befuddled Judge for a dollar.

That night, Huck goes to Jim, who claims to possess a giant, magical hairball from an ox's stomach. Huck tells Jim that he has found Pap's tracks in the snow and wants to know what his father wants. Jim says that the hairball needs money to talk, so Huck gives Jim a counterfeit quarter. Jim puts his ear to the hairball and relates that Huck's father has two angels, one black and one white, one bad and one good. It is uncertain which angel will win out, but Huck is safe for now. He will have much happiness and sorrow in his life, he will marry a poor woman and then a rich woman, and he should stay clear of the water, since that is where he will die. That night, Huck finds Pap waiting for him in his bedroom.

SUMMARY: CHAPTER V
Pap is a frightening sight. The nearly fifty-year-old man's skin is a ghastly, disgusting white. Noticing Huck's "starchy" clothes, Pap wonders out loud if Huck thinks himself better than his father and promises to take Huck "down a peg." Pap promises to teach Widow Douglas not to "meddle" and is outraged that Huck has become the first person in his family to learn to read. Pap asks if Huck is really as rich as he has heard and calls his son a liar when Huck replies that he has no more money. Pap then takes the dollar that Huck got from Judge Thatcher and leaves to buy whiskey.

The next day, Pap shows up drunk and demands Huck's money from Judge Thatcher. The Judge and Widow Douglas try to get custody of Huck but give up after the new judge in town refuses to separate a father and son. Pap eventually lands in jail after a drunken spree. The new judge takes Pap into his home and tries to reform him, but the judge and his wife prove to be very weepy and moralizing. Pap tearfully repents his ways but soon gets drunk again, and the new judge decides that the only way to reform Pap is with a shotgun.

SUMMARY: CHAPTER VI

Pap sues Judge Thatcher for Huck's fortune and continues to threaten Huck about attending school. Huck continues to attend, partly to spite his father. Pap goes on one drunken binge after another. One day, he kidnaps Huck, takes him deep into the woods to a secluded cabin on the Illinois shore, and locks Huck inside all day while he rambles outside. Eventually, Huck finds an old saw, makes a hole in the wall, and resolves to escape from both Pap and the Widow Douglas, but Pap returns as Huck is about to break free.

Pap complains that Judge Thatcher has delayed the trial to prevent him from getting Huck's wealth. He has heard that his chances of getting the money are good but that he will probably lose the fight for custody of Huck. Pap continues to rant about a mixed-race man in town; Pap is disgusted that the man is allowed to vote in his home state of Ohio, and that legally he cannot be sold into slavery until he has been in Missouri six months. Later, Pap wakes from a drunken sleep and chases after Huck with a knife, calling him the "Angel of Death" but stopping when he passes out. Huck holds a rifle pointed at his sleeping father and waits.

ANALYSIS: CHAPTERS IV–VI

In these chapters, Twain makes a number of comments on the society of his time and its attempts at reform. We see a number of well-meaning individuals who engage in foolish, even cruel behavior. The new judge in town refuses to give custody of Huck to Judge Thatcher and the Widow, despite Pap's history of neglect and abuse. This poorly informed decision not only makes us question the wisdom and morality of these public figures but also resonates with the plight of slaves in Southern society at the time. The new judge in town returns Huck to Pap because he privileges Pap's "rights" over Huck's welfare—just as slaves, because they were considered property, were regularly returned to their legal owners, no matter how badly these owners abused them. Twain also takes the opportunity to mock the bleeding-heart do-gooders of the temperance, or anti-alcohol, movement: the judge is clearly naïve, misguided, and blind to the larger evils around them, and the weeping and moralizing that goes on in his home is grating, to say the least.

Throughout these chapters, Huck is at the center of countless failures and breakdowns in the society around him, yet he maintains his characteristic resilience. Indeed, Huck's family, the legal system, and the community all fail to protect him or to provide a set of beliefs and values that are consistent and satisfying to him. Huck's wrongful imprisonment elicits sympathy and concern on our part, even though this imprisonment does not seem to distress Huck in the least. Sadly, Huck is so used to social abuses by this point in his life that he has no reason to prefer one set of abuses over the other. Likewise, although Pap is a hideous, hateful man in nearly every respect, Huck does not immediately abandon him when given the chance. Pap is, after all, Huck's father, and Huck is still a fairly young boy. Ultimately, Pap's kidnapping of Huck provides an opportunity for Huck to break from this society that has done him harm.

Pap, the embodiment of pure evil, is one of Twain's most memorable characters. Because we have no background information to explain his present state, his role is primarily symbolic. The deathly pallor of his skin, which is nauseating to Huck, makes Pap emblematic of whiteness. Unfortunately, Pap represents the worst of white society: he is illiterate, ignorant, violent, and profoundly racist. The mixed-race man who visits the town contrasts Pap in every way: he is a clean-cut, knowledgeable, and seemingly politically conscious professor. In establishing the contrast between Pap and the mixed-race man, Twain overturns traditional symbolism of his time and implies that whiteness, not blackness, is associated with evil. Jim's vision of Pap's two angels and Huck's two future wives extends this sense of confusion over good and bad, human and inhuman, right and wrong in Huck's world. At this point, Jim is unclear as to which will win, and even less clear about which *should* win.

CHAPTERS VII–X

SUMMARY: CHAPTER VII

Unaware of his earlier drunken rage, Pap wakes up and sends Huck out to check to see if any fish have been caught on the lines out in the river. Huck finds a canoe drifting in the river and hides it in the woods. When Pap leaves for the day, Huck finishes sawing his way out of the cabin. He puts food, cookware, and everything else of value from the cabin into the canoe. He then covers up the hole he cut in the wall and shoots a wild pig outside. Huck smashes the cabin door with an ax, cuts the pig's throat so it bleeds onto the cabin's dirt floor, and makes other preparations to make it seem as if robbers have broken into the cabin and killed him. Huck goes to the canoe and waits for the moon to rise, planning to paddle to Jackson's Island out in the river. Huck falls asleep and wakes to see Pap rowing by. Once Pap has passed, Huck quietly sets out downriver. He pulls into Jackson's Island, careful not to be seen.

SUMMARY: CHAPTER VIII

The next morning, a ferryboat passes Jackson Island, carrying Pap, Judge Thatcher and his daughter Bessie (known as Becky Thatcher in Tom Sawyer), Tom Sawyer, Tom's aunt Polly, some of Huck's young friends, and "plenty more" on board, all discussing Huck's apparent murder. They shoot cannonballs over the water and float loaves of bread with mercury inside, in hopes of finding Huck's corpse. Huck, still hiding carefully, catches one of the loaves and eats it. He is pleased that they are using such high-quality bread to search for him, but he feels guilty that his disappearance has upset the Widow Douglas and the others who care about him.

Huck spends three peaceful, lonely days on the island, living on plentiful berries and fish and able to smoke whenever he wishes. He spends his nights counting ferryboats and stars on the tranquil river. On the fourth day, while exploring the island, Huck is delighted to find Jim, who at first thinks Huck is a ghost. Huck is pleased that he will not be alone on the island but shocked when Jim explains that he has run away. Jim says that he overheard Miss Watson discussing selling him for $800 to a slave trader who would take him to New Orleans, separating him from his family. Jim left before Miss Watson had a chance to decide whether or not to sell him. Jim and Huck discuss superstitions—in which Jim is well-versed—and Jim's failed investments, most of which have been scams. Jim is not too disappointed by his failures, since he still has his hairy arms and chest, which, according to his superstitions, are a sign of future wealth.

SUMMARY: CHAPTER IX

In order to make a hiding place should visitors arrive on the island, Jim and Huck take the canoe and provisions into a large cave in the middle of the island. Jim predicts that it will rain, and soon a storm blows in. The two safely wait it out inside the cave. The river floods, and a washed-out house floats down the river past the island. Inside, Jim and Huck find the body of a man who has been shot in the back. Jim prevents Huck from looking at the "ghastly" face. Jim and Huck make off with some odds and ends from the houseboat.

Huck has Jim hide in the bottom of the canoe so that he won't be seen, and they make it back to the island safely.

Summary: Chapter X

Huck wonders about the dead man, but Jim warns that it's bad luck to think about such things. Huck has already incurred bad luck, according to Jim, by finding and handling a snake's shed skin. Sure enough, bad luck comes: as a joke, Huck puts a dead rattlesnake near Jim's sleeping place, and its mate comes and bites Jim. Jim's leg swells but gets better after several days. A while later, Huck decides to go ashore to get information. Jim agrees, but has Huck disguise himself as a girl, using one of the dresses they took from the houseboat. Huck practices his girl impersonation and then sets out for the Illinois shore. In a formerly abandoned shack, he finds a woman who looks about forty years old and appears to be a newcomer to the town. Huck is relieved because, as a newcomer, the woman will not be able to recognize him. Still, he resolves to remember that he is pretending to be a girl.

Analysis: Chapters VII–X

Despite Twain's disdain for the romantic, sentimentalized novels, these chapters are a tightly constructed mix of the romantic and the practical. Huck and Jim's meeting on the island begins the main story arc of the novel. Huck and Jim, both alienated from society in fundamental ways, find themselves sharing a pastoral, dreamlike setting: a safe, peaceful island where food is abundant. From this point in the novel forward, their fates are linked. Jim has had no more say in his own fate as an adult than Huck has had as a child. Both in peril, Huck and Jim have had to break with society. Freed from the hypocrisy and injustice of society, they find themselves in what seems a paradise, smoking a pipe, watching the river, and feasting on catfish and wild berries.

Two episodes in these chapters, however, remind Huck and Jim of the looming threat from outside and give us the sense that this fantasy on the island is unlikely to last. The first involves the house that floats down the river past the island. The man inside the house has clearly been murdered, and the house bears other marks of human vices: playing cards, whiskey bottles, and obscene graffiti. Although Huck and Jim gather some useful goods from the house, it reminds them that Jackson's Island is not completely isolated from the outside world. The second incident involves Jim's rattlesnake bite, a direct result of a stupid prank Huck tries to play on Jim. As in the biblical Garden of Eden, snakes lurk on this island paradise and hurt people who behave unwisely. Once again, Huck and Jim are reminded that no location is safe for them.

These two incidents also flesh out some important aspects of the relationship between Huck and Jim. In the episode with the rattlesnake, Huck acts like a child, and Jim gets hurt. In both incidents, Jim uses his knowledge to benefit both of them but also seeks to protect Huck: he refuses to let Huck see the body in the floating house, for it is the body of Huck's father. Jim is an intelligent and caring adult who has escaped out of love for his family—and he displays this same caring aspect toward Huck here. While Huck's motives are equally sound, he is still a child and frequently behaves like one. In a sense, Jim and Huck together make up a sort of alternative family in an alternative place, apart from the society that has only harmed them up to this point.

CHAPTERS XI–XIII

SUMMARY: CHAPTER XI

The woman lets Huck into the shack but eyes him suspiciously. Huck introduces himself as "Sarah Williams" from Hookerville. The woman chatters about a variety of subjects and eventually gets to the topic of Huck's murder. She reveals that Pap was a suspect and that some townspeople nearly lynched him. Then, people began to suspect Jim because he ran away the same day Huck was killed. Soon, however, suspicions again turned against Pap, after he squandered on alcohol the money that the judge gave him to find Jim. Pap left town before he could be lynched, and now there is a $200 reward being offered for him. Meanwhile, there is a $300 bounty out for Jim. The woman has noticed smoke over Jackson's Island and has told her husband to look for Jim there. He plans to go there tonight with another man and a gun.

The woman looks at Huck suspiciously and asks his name. He replies, "Mary Williams." When the woman asks about the change, he tries to cover himself by saying his full name is "Sarah Mary Williams." She has him try to kill a rat by throwing a lump of lead at it, and he nearly hits the rat, increasing her suspicions. Finally, she asks him to reveal his real male identity, saying she understands that he is a runaway apprentice and claiming she will not turn him in to the authorities. Huck says his name is George Peters and describes himself as an apprentice to a mean farmer. She lets him go after quizzing him on several farm subjects to make sure he is telling the truth. She tells Huck to send for her, Mrs. Judith Loftus, if he has trouble.

Back at the island, Huck builds a decoy campfire far from the cave and then returns to the cave to tell Jim they must leave. They hurriedly pack their things and slowly ride out on a raft they found when the river flooded.

Summary: Chapter XII

Huck and Jim build a wigwam on the raft and spend a number of days drifting downriver, traveling by night and hiding by day to avoid being seen. On their fifth night out, they pass the great lights of St. Louis. The two of them "live pretty high," buying, stealing, or hunting food as they need it. They feel somewhat remorseful about the stealing, however, so they decide to give up a few items as a sort of moral sacrifice.

One stormy night, they come upon a wrecked steamboat. Against Jim's objections, Huck goes onto the wreck to loot it and have an "adventure," the way Tom Sawyer would. On the wreck, Huck overhears two robbers threatening to kill a third so that he won't "tell." One of the two robbers manages to convince the other to let their victim be drowned with the wreck. The robbers leave. Huck finds Jim and says they have to cut the robbers' boat loose to prevent them from escaping. Jim responds by telling Huck that their own raft has broken loose and floated away.

Summary: Chapter XIII

Huck and Jim head for the robbers' boat. The robbers put some stolen items in their boat but leave in order to take some more money from their victim inside the steamboat. Jim and Huck jump into the robbers' boat and head off as quietly as possible. When they are a few hundred yards away, Huck feels bad for the robbers left stranded on the wreck because, after all, he himself might end up a murderer someday. Huck and Jim find their raft and then stop so that Huck can go ashore to get help.

Once on land, Huck finds a ferry watchman and tells him his family is stranded on the *Walter Scott* steamboat wreck. Huck invents an elaborate story about how his family got on the wreck and convinces the watchman to take his ferry to help. Huck feels proud of his good deed and thinks the Widow Douglas would have approved of him helping the robbers because she often takes an interest in "rapscallions and dead beats." Jim and Huck sink the robbers' boat and then go to sleep. Meanwhile, the wreck of the *Walter Scott* drifts downstream and, although the ferryman has gone to investigate, the robbers clearly have not survived.

ANALYSIS: CHAPTERS XI–XIII

Mrs. Loftus is one of the more sincere people Huck encounters throughout the course of the novel, but her attitude toward Jim makes her goodness somewhat problematic. Mrs. Loftus is clearly a clever woman, as we see in the tests she spontaneously designs to unmask Huck. Despite her charity toward Huck, however, Mrs. Loftus and her husband are only too happy to profit from capturing Jim, and her husband plans to bring a gun to hunt Jim like an animal. Mrs. Loftus makes a clear distinction between Huck, who tells her he has run away from a mean farmer, and Jim, who has done essentially the same thing by running away from an owner who is considering selling him.

Whereas Mrs. Loftus and the rest of white society differentiate between an abused runaway slave and an abused runaway boy, Huck does not. Huck and Jim's raft becomes a sort of haven of brotherhood and equality, as both find refuge and peace from a society that has treated them poorly. The two even engage in a bit of moral philosophizing about stealing. Though their resolution to give up stealing a few items to render their other stealing less sinful seems childish, it nevertheless represents an attempt to reconcile practical and moral concerns.

The pattern of Huck's childishness getting both himself and Jim into trouble continues in these chapters, as Huck follows his boyish, Tom Sawyer–like impulses and nearly has a run-in with the robbers on the wrecked steamboat. There is no good reason why Huck and Jim should tie up to the wrecked ship, particularly at night and in a storm, but Huck is unable to resist. The two are lucky to escape, and the incident proves to be another reminder that even on the river they are not safe from the problems that plagued them at home—violence, cruelty, and powerlessness at the hands of any white adult. Huck's attempts to reconcile the situation show that he is learning, despite his initial immaturity. When Huck acts like Tom Sawyer, trouble follows, but when he acts like himself—when he seeks to interpret and react to experience in a practical manner—things generally turn out fine.

The fact that Jim sees the foolishness of many of Huck's endeavors but never restrains Huck reminds us of Jim's extremely tenuous position as an escaped slave. In a number of instances in the novel, Jim protests when Huck formulates a foolish plan, but eventually gives in to the boy. Twain never explicitly explains Jim's reasoning, but the implication is always there that Jim's caution stems from his constant fear of being caught and returned to his former owner. After all, Huck, though a child, is a free, white child who could turn in Jim at any time and collect a large reward for doing so. Although this idea seems never to cross Huck's mind, it lurks beneath the surface of Jim and Huck's interactions and reminds us of the constant fear Jim lives with as an escaped slave.

Chapters XIV–XVI

Summary: Chapter XIV

Jim and Huck find a number of valuables among the robbers' bounty from the *Walter Scott,* mostly books, clothes, and cigars. As they relax in the woods and wait for nightfall before traveling again, Huck reads books from the wreck, and the two discuss what Huck calls their "adventures." Jim says he doesn't enjoy adventures, as they could easily end in his death or capture. Huck astonishes Jim with stories of kings, first reading from books and then adding some of his own, made-up stories. Jim had only heard of King Solomon, whom he considers a fool for wanting to chop a baby in half. Huck cannot convince Jim otherwise. Huck tells Jim about the dauphin (whom Huck mistakenly calls the "dolphin"), the son of the executed King Louis XVI of France. The dauphin currently is rumored to be wandering America. Jim refuses to believe that the French do not speak English, as Huck explains. Huck tries to argue the point with Jim but gives up in defeat.

Summary: Chapter XV

Huck and Jim approach the Ohio River, their goal. One foggy night, Huck, in the canoe, gets separated from Jim and the raft. He tries to paddle back to the raft, but the fog is so thick that he loses all sense of direction. After a lonely time adrift, Huck reunites with Jim, who is asleep on the raft. Jim is thrilled to see Huck alive, but Huck tries to trick Jim by pretending that Jim dreamed up their entire separation. Jim tells Huck the story of his dream, making the fog and the troubles he faced on the raft into an allegory of their journey to the free states. But soon Jim notices all the debris, dirt, and tree branches that collected on the raft while it was adrift. He gets mad at Huck for making a fool of him after he had worried about him so much. "It was fifteen minutes before I could work myself up to go and humble myself to a nigger," Huck says, but he eventually apologizes and does not regret it. He feels bad about hurting Jim.

SUMMARY: CHAPTER XVI

Jim and Huck worry that they will miss Cairo, the town at the mouth of the Ohio River, which runs into the free states. Meanwhile, Huck's conscience troubles him deeply about helping Jim escape from his "rightful owner," Miss Watson, especially after all she has done for Huck. Jim talks on and on about going to the free states, especially about his plan to earn money to buy the freedom of his wife and children. If their masters refuse to give up Jim's family, Jim plans to have some abolitionists kidnap them. When Huck and Jim think they see Cairo, Huck goes out on the canoe to check, having secretly resolved to give Jim up. But Huck's heart softens when he hears Jim call out that Huck is his only friend, the only one to keep a promise to him.

Huck comes upon some men in a boat who want to search his raft for escaped slaves. Huck pretends to be grateful, saying no one else would help them. He leads the men to believe that his family is on board the raft and is suffering from smallpox. The men, fearing infection, back away and tell Huck to go further downstream and lie about his family's condition to get help. Out of pity, they leave Huck forty dollars in gold. Huck feels bad because he thinks he has done wrong in not giving Jim up. However, he realizes he would feel just as bad if he had given Jim up. Huck re solves to disregard morality in the future and do what's "handiest."

Floating along, Huck and Jim pass several towns and worry that they have passed Cairo in the fog. They stop for the night and resolve to take the canoe upriver but in the morning discover that it has been stolen. They attribute the canoe's disappearance to continued bad luck from the snakeskin on Jackson's Island. Later, a steamboat collides with the raft, breaking it apart. Jim and Huck dive off in time but are separated. Huck makes it ashore, but a pack of dogs corners him.

ANALYSIS: CHAPTERS XIV–XVI

We see in these chapters that Huck, though open-minded, still largely subscribes to the Southern white conception of the world. When Jim assesses their "adventure," Huck does admit that he has acted foolishly and jeopardized Jim's safety, but he qualifies his assessment by adding that Jim is smart—for a black person. Huck also genuinely struggles with the question of whether or not to turn over Jim to the white men who ask if he is harboring any runaway slaves. In some sense, Huck still believes that turning Jim in would be the "right" thing to do, and he struggles with the idea that Miss Watson is a slave owner yet still seems to be a "good" person. Over the course of these chapters, as he spends more time with Jim, Huck is forced to question the facts that white society has taught him and that he has taken for granted.

The arguments Huck and Jim have over Huck's stories provide remarkable mini-allegories about slavery and race. When Huck tells the tale of King Solomon, who threatened to chop a baby in half, Jim argues that Solomon had so many children that he became unable to value human life properly. Huck's comments lead us to compare Jim's assessment of Solomon with whites' treatments of blacks at the time—as infinitely replaceable bodies, indistinguishable from one another. Later, Huck tells Jim that people in France don't speak English. Huck tries to convince the skeptical Jim by pointing out that cats and cows don't "talk" the same, and that, by analogy, neither should French people and American people. Jim points out that both are men and that the analogy is inappropriate. Although Jim is misinformed in a sense, he is correct in his assessment of Huck's analogy. Jim's argument provides yet another subtle reminder that, in American society at the time, not all men are treated as men. Although Jim's discussion with Huck shows that both have clever minds, we see that Jim is less imprisoned by conventional wisdom than Huck, who has grown up at least partly in mainstream white society.

We see the moral and societal importance of Huck and Jim's journey in Huck's profound moral crisis about whether he should return Jim to Miss Watson. In the viewpoint of Southern white society, Huck has effectively stolen $800—the price the slave trader has offered for Jim—from Miss Watson. However, Jim's comment that Huck is the only white man ever to keep his word to him shows that Huck has been treating Jim not as a slave but as a man. This newfound knowledge, along with Huck's guilt, keep Huck from turning Jim in. Huck realizes that he would have felt worse for doing the "right" thing and turning Jim in than he does for not turning Jim in. When Huck reaches this realization, he makes a decision to reject conventional morality in favor of what his conscience dictates. This decision represents a big step in Huck's development, as he realizes that his conscience may be a better guide than the dictates of the white society in which he has been raised.

Chapters XVII–XIX

Summary: Chapter XVII

A man calls off the dogs, saving Huck, who introduces himself as "George Jackson." The man invites "George" into his house, where the hosts express an odd suspicion that Huck is a member of a family called the Shepherdsons. Eventually, Huck's hosts decide that he is not a Shepherdson. The lady of the house tells Buck, a boy about Huck's age, to get Huck some dry clothes. Buck says he would have killed a Shepherdson had there been any Shepherdsons present. Buck tells Huck a riddle, but Huck does not understand the concept of riddles. Buck says Huck must stay with him and they will have great fun. Huck, meanwhile, invents an elaborate story to explain how he was orphaned.

Buck's family, the Grangerfords, offer to let Huck stay with them for as long as he likes. Huck innocently admires the house and its humorously tacky finery, including the work of a deceased daughter, Emmeline, who created unintentionally funny sentimental artwork and poems about people who died. Settling in with the Grangerfords and enjoying their kindness, Huck thinks that "nothing couldn't be better" than life at the comfortable house.

Summary: Chapter XVIII

> *Other places do seem so cramped up and smothery,*
> *but a raft don't. You feel mighty free and easy and*
> *comfortable on a raft.* (*See* QUOTATIONS, *p. 59*)

Huck admires Colonel Grangerford, the master of the house, and his supposed gentility. A warmhearted man, the colonel owns a very large estate with over a hundred slaves. Everyone in the household treats the colonel with great courtesy. The Grangerford children include Bob, the oldest; then Tom; then Charlotte, age twenty-five; Sophia, age twenty; and finally Buck. All of them are beautiful.

One day, Buck tries to shoot a young man named Harney Shepherdson but misses. Huck asks why Buck wanted to kill Harney, and Buck explains that the Grangerfords are in a feud with a neighboring clan of families, the Shepherdsons. No one can remember how or why the feud started, but in the last year, two people have been killed, including a fourteen-year-old Grangerford. The two families attend church together and hold their rifles between their knees as the minister preaches about brotherly love.

After church one day, Sophia Grangerford has Huck retrieve a copy of the Bible from the pews. She is delighted to find inside a note with the words "Half-past two" written on it. Later, Huck's slave valet leads Huck deep into the swamp and tells Huck he wants to show him some water-moccasins. Huck finds Jim there, much to his surprise. Jim says that he followed Huck to the shore the night they were wrecked but did not dare call out for fear of being caught. Some slaves found the raft, but Jim reclaimed it by threatening the slaves and telling them that it belonged to his white master.

The next day, Huck learns that Sophia Grangerford has run off with Harney Shepherdson. In the woods, Huck finds Buck and a nineteen-year-old Grangerford in a gunfight with the Shepherdsons. Both of the Grangerfords are killed. Deeply disturbed, Huck heads for Jim and the raft, and the two shove off downstream.

SUMMARY: CHAPTER XIX

Huck and Jim continue down the river. On one of his solo expeditions in the canoe, Huck comes upon two men on shore fleeing some trouble and begging to be let onto the raft. Huck takes them a mile downstream to safety. One man is about seventy, bald, with whiskers, and the other about thirty. Both men's clothes are badly tattered. The men do not know each other but are in similar predicaments. The younger man used to sell a paste that was meant to remove tartar from teeth but that took off much of the enamel with it. He fled to avoid the locals' ire. The older man used to run a temperance revival meeting but had to flee after word got out that he drank.

Having heard each other's stories, the two men, both professional con artists, decide to team up. The younger man declares himself an impoverished English duke and gets Huck and Jim to wait on him and treat him like royalty. The old man then reveals his true identity as the dauphin, the long lost son of King Louis XVI of France. Huck and Jim then wait on the men and call them "Duke" and "Your Majesty," respectively. Huck quickly realizes that the two men are liars, but to prevent "quarrels," he does not let on that he knows.

ANALYSIS: CHAPTERS XVII–XIX

Huck's stay at the Grangerfords represents another instance of Twain poking fun at American tastes and at the conceits of romantic literature. For Huck, who has never really had a home aside from the Widow Douglas's rather spartan house, the Grangerford house looks like a palace. Huck's admiration is genuine but naïve, for the Grangerfords and their place are somewhat absurd. In the figure of deceased Emmeline Grangerford, Twain pokes fun at Victorian literature's propensity for mourning and melancholy. Indeed, Emmeline's hilariously awful artwork and poems mock popular works of the time. The combination of overzealous bad taste and inherently sad subject matter in Emmeline's art is both bizarre and comical: as we learn, Emmeline was so enthusiastic in her artistic pursuits that she usually beat the undertaker to a new corpse. Huck, meanwhile, feels uneasy about the macabre aspect of Emmeline's work. His attempts to accept her art and life remind us that sometimes laughter is insensitive: Emmeline and her subjects were all real people who died, after all.

The great Grangerford-Shepherdson feud is yet another conceit taken from romantic literature, specifically that literature's concern with family honor. The Grangerfords and Shepherdsons are rather like Tom Sawyer grown up and armed with weapons: motivated by a sense of style and this ridiculous notion of family honor, they actually kill each other. However comical the feud is in general, though, Buck's death is a terrible moment, and Twain's tone turns entirely serious at this point. Before fleeing, Huck pulls Buck's body from the river and cries as he covers his friend's face. Twain uses this incident to comment on all systems of belief that deny another group of people their humanity. While this section of *Huckleberry Finn* is undeniably humorous, it also demonstrates how confused Huck's world is. Like so many other people Huck meets in the novel, the Grangerfords are a mix of contradictions: although they treat Huck well, they own slaves and behave more foolishly than almost anyone else in the novel.

Jim's reemergence on the raft and the encounter with the duke and the dauphin illustrate the shifting power dynamics between blacks and whites as Huck and Jim move further down the river. Jim's use of Huck's whiteness to threaten his fellow black men shows how corrupting racism and the slave system can be. We should remember that although Jim acts maliciously, he does so to protect his own freedom, which makes it difficult to judge his actions harshly. Shortly afterward, the encounter with the duke and the dauphin reminds Huck and Jim of their relative powerlessness. Although the duke and the dauphin are criminals, they are free, adult, white men who have the power to turn in both Huck and Jim. Despite Huck's feeling that one is "mighty free and easy and comfortable on a raft," the outside world and its evils remain a firmly established presence on the river. As Huck and Jim travel further, the Mississippi becomes a source of foreboding rather than freedom, a conduit toward the American "heart of darkness"—the plantations of the Deep South.

Chapters XX–XXII

Summary: Chapter XX

The duke and the dauphin ask whether Jim is a runaway slave. Huck makes up a story about how he was orphaned and tells them that he and Jim have been forced to travel at night since so many people stopped his boat to ask whether Jim was a runaway. That night, the duke and the dauphin take Huck's and Jim's beds while Huck and Jim stand watch against a storm.

The next morning, the duke gets the dauphin to agree to put on a performance of Shakespeare in the next town they pass. They reach the town and find that everyone in the town has left for a religious revival meeting in the woods, a lively affair with several thousand people singing and shouting. The dauphin gets up and tells the crowd that he is a former pirate, now reformed by the revival meeting, who will return to the Indian Ocean as a missionary. The crowd joyfully takes up a collection, netting the dauphin more than eighty dollars and many kisses from pretty young women.

Meanwhile, the duke takes over the deserted print office in town and earns nearly ten dollars selling print jobs, subscriptions, and advertisements in the local newspaper. The duke also prints up a "handbill," or leaflet, offering a reward for Jim's capture, which will allow them to travel freely by day and tell anyone who inquires that Jim is their captive. Meanwhile, Jim has been innocently trying to get the dauphin to speak French, but the supposed heir to the French throne claims that he has forgotten the language.

Summary: Chapter XXI

Waking up after a night of drinking, the duke and dauphin practice the balcony scene from *Romeo and Juliet* and the swordfight from *Richard III* on the raft. The duke also works on his recitation of the "To be, or not to be" soliloquy from *Hamlet*, which he doesn't know well at all, throwing in lines from other parts of *Hamlet* and even some lines from *Macbeth*. To Huck, however, the duke seems to possess a great talent.

Next, the group visits a one-horse town in Arkansas where lazy young men loiter in the streets, arguing over chewing tobacco. Huck gives a detailed, absurd description of the town. The duke posts handbills for the theatrical performance, and Huck witnesses the shooting of a rowdy drunk by a man, Sherburn, whom the drunk has insulted. The shooting takes place in front of the victim's daughter. A crowd gathers around the dying man and then goes off to lynch Sherburn.

SUMMARY: CHAPTER XXII

The lynch mob charges through the streets, proceeds to Sherburn's house, and knocks down the front fence. The crowd quickly backs away, however, as Sherburn greets them from the roof of his front porch, rifle in hand. After a chilling silence, Sherburn delivers a haughty speech on human nature in which he attacks the cowardice and mob mentality of the average person. Sherburn tells the crowd that no one will lynch him in the daytime. The mob, chastened, disperses.

Huck then goes to the circus, a "splendid" show with a quick-witted clown. A performer, pretending to be a drunk, forces himself into the ring and tries to ride a horse, apparently hanging on for dear life. The crowd roars in amusement, except for Huck, who cannot bear to watch the poor man in danger. That night, only twelve people attend the duke's performance, and they jeer throughout the entire show. The duke then prints another handbill, this time advertising a performance of The King's Cameleopard [Giraffe] or The Royal Nonesuch. Bold letters across the bottom read, "Women and Children Not Admitted."

ANALYSIS: CHAPTERS XX–XXII

Although these chapters involving the duke and the dauphin appear purely comic on the surface, a dark commentary undercuts the comedy in virtually every episode. On the surface, the duke and the dauphin seem to be just two bumbling con artists, but they present an immediate threat to Huck and Jim. The two men constantly and cruelly toy with Jim's precarious status as a runaway slave and even use this fact to their own advantage when they print the fake leaflet advertising a reward for Jim's capture. Moreover, the fact that the duke and the dauphin run their first scam at a sacred event—a religious meeting—demonstrates their incredible malice. At the same time, however, it also suggests that the religious revival meeting may be as much of a scam as any of the "royal" pair's shenanigans. Continuing the pattern that we have seen throughout *Huckleberry Finn,* nearly everyone Huck and Jim encounter on the river is an unsavory character or a fake in one way or another.

Sherburn's murder of the drunk and the subsequent mob scene continue this vein of simultaneous absurdity and seriousness in the novel and contribute to the sense of moral confusion in the town. Although Sherburn's shooting of the drunk is cold-blooded, his speech to the angry mob is among the most profound meditations on human nature in *Huckleberry Finn.* Sherburn's criticisms of the cowardice and despicable behavior of his fellow citizens are accurate, and his eloquence is impressive. Furthermore, much of what he has to say about cowardice relates directly to the deplorable behavior of the people of St. Petersburg, which has put Huck and Jim in peril in the first place. All the while, however, we are aware that this thoughtful speech comes from the mouth of a man who has just shot a defenseless drunk. Like Huck, we are confused and disoriented.

Rather than provide some relief from this world of malice and chaos, Huck's leisurely trip to the circus only complicates matters further. Coming between the religious revival and the con men's performance, the circus illustrates just how fine the line is between spiritually enriching experience, legitimate entertainment, and downright fraud. Huck's concern for the seemingly drunk horseman is an elegantly constructed ending to this set of chapters. In a world like the one Twain depicts in the novel, one can no longer distinguish between reality and fakery, doom and deliverance.

Chapters XXIII–XXV

Summary: Chapter XXIII

The Royal Nonesuch plays to a capacity audience. The dauphin, who appears onstage wearing nothing aside from body paint and some "wild" accoutrements, has the audience howling with laughter. But the crowd nearly attacks the duke and the dauphin when they end the show after only a brief performance. The people in the crowd, embarrassed at having been ripped off, decide to protect their honor by making certain that *everyone* in the town gets ripped off. After the performance, they tell everyone else in town that the play was wonderful. The second night, therefore, also brings a capacity crowd.

As the duke has anticipated, the crowd on the third night consists of the two previous nights' audiences coming to get their revenge. Huck and the duke make a getaway to the raft before the show starts. They have earned $465 over the three-night run. Jim is shocked that the royals are such "rapscallions." Huck explains that history shows nobles to be rapscallions who constantly lie, steal, and decapitate, but his history knowledge is factually very questionable.

Huck does not see the point in telling Jim that the duke and the dauphin are fakes. Jim spends his night watches "moaning and mourning" for his wife and two children. Though "it don't seem natural," Huck concludes that Jim loves his family as much as white men love theirs. Jim is torn apart when he hears a thud in the distance that reminds him of the time he beat his daughter Lizabeth for not doing what he told her to do. When he was beating her, Jim didn't realize that Lizabeth couldn't hear his instructions because a bout with scarlet fever had left her deaf.

SUMMARY: CHAPTER XXIV

As the duke and the dauphin tie up the raft to work over another town, Jim complains about having to wait, frightened, in the boat, tied up as a runaway slave in order to avoid suspicion, while the others are gone. In response, the duke disguises Jim in a calico stage robe and blue face paint and posts a sign on him that reads, "Sick Arab—but harmless when not out of his head." The dauphin, dressed up in his newly bought clothes, decides he wants to make a big entrance into the next town, so he and Huck board a steamboat docked several miles above the town.

The dauphin encounters a talkative young man who tells him about a recently deceased local man, Peter Wilks. Wilks had recently sent for his two brothers from Sheffield, England—Harvey, whom Peter had not seen since they were boys, and William, who is deaf and mute. Wilks left much of his property to these brothers when he died, but it seems uncertain whether they will ever arrive. The dauphin wheedles the young traveler, who is en route to South America, to provide him with details concerning the Wilks family.

Arriving in Wilks's hometown, the duke and the dauphin ask for Wilks and feign anguish when told of his death. The dauphin even makes strange hand gestures to the duke, feigning sign language. The scene is enough to make Huck "ashamed of the human race."

SUMMARY: CHAPTER XXV

A crowd gathers before the Wilks home to watch Wilks's three nieces tearfully greet the duke and the dauphin, whom they believe to be their English uncles. The entire town then joins in the "blubbering." Huck has "never seen anything so disgusting." The letter Wilks has left behind bequeaths the house and $3,000 to his nieces. His brothers stand to inherit another $3,000, along with more than double that amount in real estate. After finding Wilks's money in the basement, where the letter had said it would be, the duke and the dauphin privately count the money. They add $415 of their own money when they discover that the stash comes up short of the letter's promised $6,000. Then, they hand all the money over to the Wilks sisters in a great show before a crowd of townspeople. Doctor Robinson, an old friend of the deceased, interrupts to declare the duke and the dauphin frauds, noting that their accents are ridiculously phony. He asks Mary Jane, the eldest Wilks sister, to listen to him as a friend and dismiss the impostors. In reply, Mary Jane hands the dauphin the $6,000 to invest as he sees fit.

ANALYSIS: CHAPTERS XXIII–XXV

Although the duke and the dauphin become increasingly malicious and cruel in their scams, Twain continues to portray the victims of the con men's schemes as unflatteringly as the con men themselves. The duke and the dauphin's production of The Royal Nonesuch, for example, is a complete farce, a brief, insubstantial show for which the audience is grossly overcharged. But what makes the con men's show a real success, however, is not any ingenuity on their part— they are as inept as ever—but rather the audience's own selfishness and vindictiveness. Rather than warn the other townspeople that the show was terrible, the first night's ticketholders would rather see everyone else get ripped off in the same way they did. Thus, the con men's scheme becomes even more successful because the townspeople display vindictiveness rather than selflessness. In much the same way, the cruel scheme to steal the Wilks family's inheritance succeeds only because of the stupidity and gullibility of the Wilks sisters, particularly Mary Jane. Admittedly, the grieving Wilks sisters likely are not in the best frame of mind to think rationally after their loss. Nonetheless, despite the fact that the duke and the dauphin are hilariously inept in their role-playing and fake in their accents, the only person who even begins to suspect them is Doctor Robinson— and Mary Jane dismisses his advice without a thought. But even the Doctor comes across as annoyingly self-righteous. Together, these episodes contribute to the overall sense of moral confusion in the world of *Huckleberry Finn*. Although the con men's audacity and maliciousness are sometimes shocking, Twain's portrayal of the victims is often equally unsympathetic.

Jim, meanwhile, displays an honest sensitivity that contrasts him ever more strongly with the debased white characters who surround him. Jim bares himself emotionally to Huck, expressing a poignant longing for his family and admitting his errors as a father when he tells of the time he beat his daughter when she did not deserve it. Jim's willingness to put himself in a vulnerable position and admit his failings to Huck adds a new dimension of humanity to his character. Jim's nobility becomes even more apparent when we recall that he has been willing to forgive others throughout the novel, even though he is unable to forgive himself for one honest mistake. As we see in these chapters, Jim's honesty and emotional openness have a profound effect on Huck. Having been brought up among racist white assumptions, Huck is surprised to see that ties of familial love can be as strong among blacks as among whites. Although Huck's development is still incomplete—he still qualifies his observations a bit, noting that it doesn't seem "natural" for Jim to be so attached to his family—his mind is open and he clearly views Jim more as a human and less as a slave.

Chapters XXVI–XXVIII

Summary: Chapter XXVI

The dauphin arranges to stay in the Wilks house. Huck has supper with Joanna, the youngest Wilks sister, whom he calls "the hare-lip" because of her cleft lip, a birth defect. Joanna tests Huck's knowledge of England, and he makes several slips, forgetting that he is supposedly from Sheffield and that the dauphin is supposed to be a Protestant minister. Finally, Joanna asks if he has made the entire thing up. Joanna's sisters, Mary Jane and Susan, interrupt and instruct Joanna to be courteous to their guest, and she graciously apologizes. Huck feels terrible about letting such sweet women be swindled and resolves to get them their money back. He goes to the con men's room to search for the money and hides when they enter. The duke wants to leave town that night, but the dauphin convinces him to stay until they have stolen all the family's property. After the men leave the room, Huck finds the $6,000 in gold, takes it to his sleeping cubby, and then sneaks out late at night.

Summary: Chapter XXVII

Huck hides the sack of money in Peter Wilks's coffin as Mary Jane, crying, enters the front room where her dead father's body lies. Huck, who doesn't get another opportunity to remove the money safely, worries about what will happen to it. The next day, a dog barking in the cellar disrupts the funeral. The undertaker slips out and returns after a "whack" is heard from downstairs. In a voice that everyone present can hear, he whispers that the dog has caught a rat. In the next moment, though, Huck watches with horror as the undertaker seals the coffin without looking inside. Huck realizes he will never know whether the duke and the dauphin have gotten the money back. He wonders if he should write to Mary Jane after he has left town to tell her to have the coffin dug up.

Saying he will take the Wilks girls to England, the dauphin sells off the estate and the slaves, sending a slave mother to New Orleans and her two sons to Memphis. The scene at the grief-stricken family's separation is heart-rending, and the Wilks women are upset. Huck comforts himself with the knowledge that the slave family will be reunited in a week or so when the duke and the dauphin are exposed. When the con men question Huck about the missing money, he manages to make them think the Wilks family slaves were responsible for the disappearance.

Summary: Chapter XXVIII

The next morning, Huck finds Mary Jane crying in her bedroom. All her joy about the trip to England has given way to distress over the separation of the slave family. Touched, Huck unthinkingly blurts out that the family will be reunited in less than two weeks. Mary Jane, overjoyed, asks Huck to explain. Huck feels uneasy, for he has little experience telling the truth while in a predicament. He tells Mary Jane the truth but asks her to wait at a friend's house until later that night in order to give him time to get away, because the fate of another person (Jim) also hangs in the balance. Huck instructs Mary Jane to leave without seeing her "uncles," for her innocent face would give away their secret. Huck leaves her a note with the location of the money. She promises to remember him forever and to pray for him. In retrospect, Huck tells us that he has never seen Mary Jane since but that he thinks of her often.

Shortly after Mary Jane leaves the house, Huck encounters Susan and Joanna and tells them that their sister has gone to see a sick friend. Joanna cross-examines him about this, but he manages to trick them into staying quiet about the whole thing. Later that day, a mob interrupts the auction of the family's possessions. Among the mob are two men who claim to be the real Harvey and William Wilks.

Analysis: Chapters XXVI–XXVIII

These chapters mark several milestones in Huck's development, as he acts on his conscience for the first time and takes concrete steps to thwart the schemes of the duke and the dauphin. Although Huck has shown an increasing maturity and sense of morality as the novel has progressed, he has been tentative in taking sides or action, frequently hedging his bets and qualifying the statements he makes. He has chosen not to challenge or expose the duke and the dauphin even though he has been aware from the start that they are frauds. Earlier, watching as the con men scam the Wilks sisters in Chapter XXIV, Huck tells him that the sight makes him ashamed to be part of the human race. Though this strong statement is, in itself, a step for Huck, he does not act on it until now. The first concrete action Huck takes is his retrieval of the $6,000 in gold, which he places in Wilks's coffin.

Despite these developments, however, Huck still has several lessons to learn and still struggles with the conflicting messages he receives from society and from his personal experiences. Even though Huck rightly takes the money from the con men, he does not give it to the Wilks sisters directly, and he still cannot bring himself to expose the con men to the Wilkses. It is not until two chapters later that Huck, seeing Mary Jane crying in her bedroom, blurts out that the duke and the dauphin are frauds. Also, Huck seems relatively unfazed when he hears that the dauphin's plan to liquidate the Wilks's property will require the separation of a slave woman from her children. Huck confesses to Mary Jane not because he is upset about the splitting of the slave family but because he feels bad that she is upset about it. Twain implies, through Huck's struggle with the issue, that the attitudes and assumptions that enable racism and slavery in the South are deep-seated and difficult to overcome. Although Huck has made great strides, he still struggles to make sense of the confusing world around him. His predicament is understandable: after all, a world in which both seemingly good people (Miss Watson) and clearly evil people (the duke and the dauphin) are willing to perpetrate great cruelty—separating a mother from her children—is a confusing world indeed.

Although these chapters are generally serious in tone, Twain maintains his characteristic mix of absurdity, suspense, humor, and biting cynicism throughout. The funeral scene is one of Twain's brilliant comic set pieces, complete with screechy music, blubbering mourners, and a smarmy undertaker, all of which enable Huck to make wry observations about human nature while he sweats out the fate of the money he has hidden in the coffin. Then, the climactic appearance of an alternate set of Wilks brothers at the end of Chapter XXVIII sets the stage for more absurdity and confrontation. The remarkable mix of serious social commentary and entertaining suspense and humor is what Twain is perhaps best known for—and what has made *The Adventures of Huckleberry Finn* such an enduring work.

Chapters XXIX–XXXI

Summary: Chapter XXIX

The real Harvey Wilks, in an authentic English accent, explains the reasons he and his brother, William, were delayed: their luggage was misdirected, and his mute brother broke his arm, leaving him unable to communicate by signs. Doctor Robinson again declares the duke and the dauphin to be frauds and has the crowd bring the real and the fraudulent Wilks brothers to a tavern for examination. The frauds draw suspicion when they fail to produce the $6,000 from the Wilks inheritance.

A lawyer friend of the deceased then asks the duke, the dauphin, and the real Harvey to sign a piece of paper. When the lawyer compares the writing samples to letters he has from the real Harvey, the frauds are exposed. The dauphin, however, refuses to give up and claims that the duke is playing a joke on everyone by disguising his handwriting. Because the real William serves as scribe for the real Harvey and cannot write due to his broken arm, the crowd cannot prove that the real Wilkses are indeed who they say they are. To put an end to the situation, the real Harvey declares he knows of a tattoo on his brother's chest, asking the undertaker who dressed the body to back him up. But after the dauphin and Harvey each offer a different version of the tattoo's appearance, the undertaker surprises everyone by telling the crowd he saw no tattoo.

The mob cries out for the blood of all four men, but the lawyer instead sends them out to exhume the body and check for the tattoo themselves. The mob carries the four Wilks claimants and Huck with them. The mob is in an uproar when the $6,000 in gold is discovered in the coffin. In the excitement, Huck escapes. Passing the Wilks house, he notices a light in the upstairs window and thinks of Mary Jane. Huck steals a canoe and makes his way to the raft, and he and Jim shove off once again. Huck dances for joy on the raft. His heart sinks, however, when the duke and the dauphin approach in a boat.

Summary: Chapter XXX

The dauphin nearly strangles Huck out of anger at his desertion, but the duke stops him. The con men explain that they escaped after the gold was found. The duke and the dauphin each believe that the other hid the gold in the coffin to retrieve it later, without the other knowing. They nearly come to blows but eventually make up and go to sleep.

Summary: Chapter XXXI

> *It was awful thoughts and awful words, but they was said. And I let them stay said; and never thought no more about reforming.*
>
> (*See* QUOTATIONS, *p. 60*)

The foursome travels downstream on the raft for several days without stopping, trying to outdistance any rumors of the scams of the duke and the dauphin. The con men try several schemes on various towns, without success. Then, the two start to have secret discussions, worrying Jim and Huck, who resolve to ditch them at the first opportunity. Finally, the duke, the dauphin, and Huck go ashore in one town to feel out the situation. The con men get into a fight at a tavern, and Huck takes the chance to escape. Back at the raft, however, there is no sign of Jim. A boy explains that a man recognized Jim as a runaway from a handbill that offered $200 for Jim's capture in New Orleans—the same fraudulent handbill that the duke had printed earlier. The boy says that the man who captured Jim had to leave suddenly and sold his interest in the captured runaway for forty dollars to a farmer named Silas Phelps.

Based on the boy's description, Huck realizes that it was the dauphin himself who captured and quickly sold Jim. Huck decides to write to Tom Sawyer to tell Miss Watson where Jim is. But Huck soon realizes that Miss Watson would sell Jim anyway. Furthermore, as soon as Huck's part in the story got out, he would be ashamed of having helped a slave, a black man, escape. Overwhelmed by his predicament, Huck suddenly realizes that this quandary must be God's punishment for the sin of helping Jim. Huck tries to pray for forgiveness but finds he cannot because his heart is not in it. Huck writes the letter to Miss Watson. Before he starts to pray, though, he thinks of the time he spent with Jim on the river, of Jim's kind heart, and of their friendship. Huck trembles. After a minute, he decides, "All right then, I'll go to hell!" and resolves to "steal Jim out of slavery."

Huck puts on his store-bought clothes and goes to see Silas Phelps, the man who is holding Jim. While on his search, Huck encounters the duke putting up posters for The Royal Nonesuch. When the duke questions him, Huck concocts a story about how he wandered the town but found neither Jim nor the raft. The duke initially slips and reveals where Jim really is (on the Phelps farm) but then changes his story and says he sold Jim to a man forty miles away. The duke encourages Huck to head out on the three-day, forty-mile trip.

ANALYSIS: CHAPTERS XXIX–XXXI

In the aftermath of the Wilks episode, the duke and the dauphin lose the last vestiges of their inept, bumbling charm and become purely menacing and dangerous figures. Although the standoff over the Wilks estate ultimately is resolved without any physical or financial harm to anyone, the depth of greed and sliminess the con men display is astonishing. Then, just when it appears the duke and the dauphin can sink no lower, the catastrophe that Twain has foreshadowed for the last few chapters materializes when Huck discovers that Jim is missing. Just as it has throughout *The Adventures of Huckleberry Finn,* evil follows Huck and Jim onto the raft and thwarts their best attempts to escape it.

Jim's capture significantly matures Huck, for it convinces him to break with the con men for good and leads him to a second moment of moral reckoning. Huck searches the social and religious belief systems that white society has taught him for a way out of his predicament about turning Jim in. In the end, Huck is unable to pray because he cannot truly believe in these systems, for he cares too much about Jim to deny Jim's existence and humanity. Huck's thoughts of his friendship with Jim lead him to listen to his own conscience, and, echoing his sentiments from Chapter I, Huck resolves to act justly by helping Jim and "go to hell" if necessary. Once again, Huck turns received notions upside down, as he figures that even hell would be better than the society in which he lives. Huck then sets out on his first truly adult endeavor—setting off to free Jim at whatever moral or physical cost to himself. It is vital to note that Huck undertakes this action with the belief that it might send him to hell. Though he does not articulate this truth to himself, he trades his fate for Jim's and thereby accepts the life of a black man as equal to his own.

CHAPTERS XXXII–XXXV

SUMMARY: CHAPTER XXXII

With only trust in providence to help him free his friend, Huck finds the Phelps's house, where Jim is supposedly being held. A pack of hounds threatens Huck, but a slave woman calls them off. The white mistress of the house, Sally, comes outside, delighted to see Huck because she is certain he is her nephew, Tom. Sally asks why he has been delayed the last several days. Taking the opportunity to conceal his identity by pretending to be her nephew, Huck explains that a cylinder head on the steamboat blew out. When Sally asks whether anyone was hurt in the explosion, Huck says no, a "nigger" was killed. Sally expresses relief that the explosion was so "lucky."

Huck is not sure he will be able to keep up the charade as Tom. When Sally's husband, Silas, returns, however his enthusiastic greeting reveals to Huck that Sally and Silas are the aunt and uncle of none other than Tom Sawyer, Huck's best friend. Hearing a steamboat go up the river, Huck heads out to the docks, supposedly to get his luggage but really to inform Tom of the situation should he arrive.

SUMMARY: CHAPTER XXXIII

Huck meets Tom's wagon coming down the road. Tom is at first startled by the "ghost," believing that Huck was murdered back in St. Petersburg, but is eventually convinced that Huck is actually alive. Tom even agrees to help Huck free Jim. Huck is shocked by Tom's willingness to do something so wrong by society's standards: "Tom Sawyer fell considerable in my estimation," he tells us.

Tom follows Huck to the Phelps house a half-hour later. The isolated family is thrilled to have another guest. Tom introduces himself as William Thompson from Ohio, stopping on his way to visit his uncle nearby. The lively Tom leans over and kisses his aunt in the middle of dinner, and she nearly slaps the boy she thinks is an impolite stranger. Laughing, Tom pretends that he is his own half-brother, Sid. The two boys wait for Sally and Silas to mention the runaway slave supposedly being held on their property, but the adults say nothing. However, when one of Sally and Silas's boys asks to see the show that is passing through town—the duke and the dauphin's—Silas says that "the runaway" alerted him to the fact that the show was a con.

That night, Huck and Tom sneak out of the house. As they walk on the road, they see a mob of townspeople running the duke and the dauphin, tarred and feathered, out of town on a rail. Huck feels bad for the two, and his ill feelings toward them melt away. "Human beings can be awful cruel to one another," he observes. Huck concludes that a conscience is useless because it makes you feel bad no matter what you do. Tom agrees.

Summary: Chapter XXXIV

> *Tom told me what his plan was, and I see in a minute*
> *it was worth fifteen of mine for style, and would make*
> *Jim just as free a man as mine would, and maybe get us*
> *all killed besides.*   (*See* QUOTATIONS, *p. 61*)

Tom remembers seeing a black man delivering food to a shed on the Phelps property earlier that evening and deduces that the shed is where Jim is being held. His perceptive observation impresses Huck, who hatches a plan to free Jim by stealing the key to the shed and making off with Jim by night. Tom belittles this plan for its simplicity and lack of showmanship. Tom then comes up with a wild plan that Huck admits is fifteen times more stylish than his own—it might even get all three of them killed. Meanwhile, Huck finds it hard to believe that respectable Tom is going to sacrifice his reputation by helping a slave escape.

Huck and Tom get Jim's keeper, a superstitious slave, to let them see Jim. When Jim cries out in recognition, Tom protects their secret by tricking Jim's keeper into thinking the cry was the work of witches. Tom and Huck promise to dig Jim out and begin to make preparations.

Summary: Chapter XXXV

Tom, disappointed that Silas Phelps has taken so few precautions to guard Jim, proclaims that he and Huck will have to invent all the obstacles to Jim's rescue. Tom says they must saw Jim's chain off instead of just lifting it off the bed's framework, because that's how it's done in all the books. Tom rattles off a list of other things that are allegedly necessary in plotting an escape, including a rope ladder, a moat, and a shirt on which Jim can keep a journal, presumably written in his own blood. Sawing Jim's leg off to free him from the chains would also be a nice touch. But since they are pressed for time, they will dig Jim out with case-knives, or large table knives. Despite all the theft that the plan entails, Tom chastises Huck for stealing a watermelon from the slaves' garden and makes Huck give the slaves a dime as compensation.

Analysis: Chapters XXXII–XXXV

As in the early chapters of the novel, Tom Sawyer again serves as a foil to Huck in these chapters. Brash, unconcerned with others, and dependent on the "authorities" of romantic adventure novels, Tom hatches a wild plan to free Jim. Huck recognizes the foolishness and potential danger of Tom's plan and says it could get the three of them killed. It is not surprising that Tom's willingness to help free Jim confuses Huck, for Tom has always concerned himself with conforming to social expectations and preserving his own reputation. Freeing Jim would seem to be objectionable on both counts. Huck, meanwhile, though willing to trade his life and reputation for Jim, thinks of himself as a poor, worthless member of white society. Huck sees Tom's life as worth something more than that and believes that Tom has something to lose by helping to free Jim. In the end, though, we sense that Tom has no concept of the life-and-death importance of Jim's liberation but instead just views the effort simply as one big opportunity for fun and adventure.

Twain makes a scathing comment on the insidious racism of the South in the exchange between Sally and Huck about the explosion on the steamboat. When Sally asks if anyone was hurt in the explosion, Huck replies "No'm. Killed a nigger," to which Sally replies, "Well, it's lucky; because sometimes people do get hurt." It is unclear whether Huck is simply role-playing—mimicking the attitudes of an average white Southern boy in pretending to be Tom—or whether he still retains some vestiges of the racism with which he has been brought up. Sally, however, is inarguably racist in her response, saying that it's fortunate no one was hurt when she has just learned that a black man lost his life. Twain condemns this kind of automatic, offhand racism throughout the novel, but his criticism is at its most apparent here. This conversation provides yet another example of the confusing moral environment that surrounds Huck: Sally is clearly a "good" and kind woman in many traditional senses, yet she doesn't think twice about considering the loss of a black man's life no loss at all.

CHAPTERS XXXVI–XXXIX

SUMMARY: CHAPTER XXXVI

Late that night, Tom and Huck, after much fruitless effort, give up digging with the knives and switch to pick-axes instead. The next day, they gather candlesticks, spoons, and tin plates. Tom says that Jim can etch a declaration of his captivity on the tin plate using the other objects, then throw it out the window for the world to read, just like in Tom's novels. That night, the boys dig their way to Jim, who is delighted to see them. He tells them that Sally and Silas have been to visit and pray with him. Jim does not understand the boys' fancy scheme but agrees to go along. Tom convinces Jim's keeper, Nat, who believes witches are haunting him, that the only cure is to bake a "witch pie" and give it to Jim. Tom plans to bake a rope ladder into the pie.

SUMMARY: CHAPTER XXXVII

Aunt Sally notices the missing shirt, candles, sheets, and other articles Huck and Tom steal for their plan, and she takes out her anger at the disappearances on seemingly everyone except the boys. She believes that perhaps rats have stolen some of the items, so Huck and Tom secretly plug up the ratholes in the house, confounding Uncle Silas when he goes to do the same job. By removing and then replacing sheets and spoons, the boys confuse Sally so much that she loses track of how many she has. The baking of the "witch pie" is a trying task, but the boys finally finish it and send it to Jim.

SUMMARY: CHAPTER XXXVIII

Tom insists that Jim scratch an inscription bearing his coat of arms on the wall of the shed, the way the books say. Making pens from the spoons and candlestick is a great deal of trouble, but they manage. Tom creates an unintentionally humorous coat of arms and composes a set of mournful declarations for Jim to inscribe on the wall. Tom, however, expresses disapproval at the fact that they are writing on a wall made of wood rather than stone. The boys try to steal a millstone, but it proves too heavy for them, so they sneak Jim out to help. As Huck and Jim struggle with the millstone, Huck wryly notes that Tom has a talent for supervising while others do the work. Tom tries to get Jim to take a rattlesnake or rat into the shack to tame, and then tries to convince Jim to grow a flower to water with his tears. Jim protests against the unnecessary amount of trouble Tom wants to create, but Tom replies that his ideas present opportunities for greatness.

SUMMARY: CHAPTER XXXIX

Huck and Tom capture rats and snakes to put in the shed with the captive Jim and accidentally infest the Phelps house with them. Aunt Sally falls into a panic over the disorder in her household, while Jim hardly has room to move with all the wildlife in his shed. Uncle Silas, not having heard back from the plantation from which the leaflet said Jim ran away, plans to advertise Jim as a captured runaway in the New Orleans and St. Louis newspapers—the latter of which would surely reach Miss Watson in St. Petersburg. Tom, partly to thwart Silas and partly because the books he has read say to do so, puts the last part of his plan into action, writing letters from an "unknown friend" that warn of trouble to the Phelpses. The letters terrify the family. Tom finishes with a longer letter pretending to be from a member of a band of desperate gangsters who are planning to steal Jim. The letter's purported author claims to have found religion, so he wishes to offer information to help thwart the theft. The letter goes on to detail when and how the imaginary thieves will try to seize Jim.

ANALYSIS: CHAPTERS XXXVI–XXXIX

In these chapters, Tom, Huck, and Jim revert, in many ways, to the roles they played at the beginning of the novel. Tom once again gets caught up in his romantic ideas of valiantly rescuing Jim, which, though humorous, are frustrating when we see how long they delay Jim's escape. Tom gets so enmeshed in his imagination that he and Huck almost forget why they are going to so much trouble. Huck, for his part, reverts to the same follower status in relation to Tom that he held at the beginning of the novel. Normally the voice of reason and conscience in his dealings with Tom, Huck seems to have totally forgotten his principles and his friendship with Jim. Both Tom and Huck get so enthralled in their game that they seem to forget that Jim is a human being. To the boys, he becomes almost an object or a prop, to the extent that they even ask him in all seriousness to share his quarters with snakes and rats. Imprisoned in the shed, Jim is just as captive and powerless as he was before he originally escaped.

The return of this old dynamic between the boys and Jim clouds our view of the boys and of Huck's development in particular. Indeed, it seems in many ways that Huck, in his decision to follow Tom's plans, forgets many of the lessons he has learned with Jim on the raft. In a sense, Tom and Huck, in their manipulations of Jim, descend to the level of those who own or trade slaves. The boys' thoughtlessness and callousness contrast with the behavior of Aunt Sally and Uncle Silas, who, though themselves slave owners, frequently visit and pray with Jim. At the same time, however, Sally and Silas plan to return Jim to a life of imprisonment and cruelty, while the boys, despite their toying with Jim, are nevertheless trying to free him. This moral confusion becomes even deeper when we see how the boys dupe and victimize Aunt Sally as much as Jim. In the end, the moral confusion evident in these characters' interaction is so great that Twain leaves us with little basis upon which to make any substantive judgment.

CHAPTERS XL–XLIII

SUMMARY: CHAPTER XL

Aunt Sally and Uncle Silas, rattled by the mysterious letter, send Tom and Huck to bed right after supper. Later that night, Huck sees that fifteen uneasy local farmers with guns have gathered in the front room of the house. Huck goes to the shed to warn Jim and Tom, but news of the armed men only excites Tom even more. Suddenly, the men attack the shed. In the darkness, Tom, Huck, and Jim escape through the hole they cut in the wall. Tom makes a noise going over the fence, attracting the attention of the men, who shoot at the boys and Jim as they run. They make it to their canoe and set off downstream toward the island where the raft is hidden. They delight in their success, especially Tom, who has a bullet in the leg as a souvenir. Huck and Jim are concerned about Tom's wound, and Jim says they should get a doctor, since Tom would if the situation were reversed. Jim's statement confirms Huck's belief that Jim is "white inside."

SUMMARY: CHAPTER XLI

Leaving Jim and Tom on the island with the raft, Huck finds a doctor and sends him to Tom in the canoe, which only holds one person. The next morning, Huck runs into Silas, who takes him home. The place is filled with farmers and their wives, all discussing the bizarre contents of Jim's shed and the hole. They conclude that a band of robbers of amazing skill must have tricked not only the Phelpses and their friends but also the original desperadoes who sent the letter. Sally refuses to let Huck out to find Tom (who she still thinks is Sid), since she is so sad to have lost Sid and does not want to risk another boy. Huck, touched by her concern, vows never to hurt her again.

SUMMARY: CHAPTER XLII

Tom does not return, and Silas's efforts to find him end in vain. In the meantime, a letter arrives from Aunt Polly, Sally's sister. Sally casts the letter aside when she sees Tom, who she thinks is Sid. The boy is brought in semi-conscious on a mattress, accompanied by a crowd including Jim, in chains, and the doctor. Some of the local men would like to hang Jim but are unwilling to risk having to compensate Jim's master. They treat Jim roughly and chain him hand and foot inside the shed. The doctor intervenes, telling the crowd how Jim has sacrificed his freedom to help nurse Tom.

Sally, meanwhile, stays at Tom's bedside, glad that his condition has improved. Tom wakes and gleefully details how they set Jim free. Horrified to learn that Jim is now in chains, Tom explains that Miss Watson died two months ago and that her will stipulated that Jim should be set free. The old woman regretted ever having considered selling Jim down the river. Just then, Aunt Polly walks into the room. She has come to Arkansas from St. Petersburg after receiving a letter from Sally mentioning that Sid Sawyer—Tom's alias—had arrived with "Tom"—who was actually Huck. Tom has been intercepting communications between the sisters, and Polly has been forced to appear in person to sort out the confusion. After a tearful reunion with Sally, she identifies Tom and Huck and yells at both boys for their misadventures.

Summary: Chapter XLIII

> *But I reckon I got to light out for the territory ahead of the rest, because Aunt Sally she's going to adopt me and sivilize me, and I can't stand it. I been there before.* (See QUOTATIONS, p. 62)

When Huck asks Tom what he had planned to do once he had freed the already-freed Jim, Tom replies that he was planning to repay Jim for his troubles and send him back a hero, giving him a reception complete with a marching band. When Aunt Polly and the Phelpses hear about the assistance Jim gave the doctor in nursing Tom, they immediately unchain him, feed him, and treat him like a king. Tom gives Jim forty dollars for his troubles, and Jim declares that the omen of his hairy chest—which was supposed to bring him fortune—has come true.

Tom makes a full recovery and wears the bullet from his leg on a watch-guard around his neck. He and Huck would like to go on another adventure, to "Indian Territory" (present-day Oklahoma). Huck thinks it quite possible that Pap has taken all his money by now, but Jim says that could not have happened. Jim tells Huck that the dead body they found on the floating house during the flood was Pap. Huck now has nothing more to write about and is "rotten glad" about that, because writing a book turned out to be quite a task. He does not plan any future writings. Instead, he plans to head out west immediately because Aunt Sally is already trying to "sivilize" him. Huck has had quite enough of that.

Analysis: Chapters XL–XLIII

The ending of *Huckleberry Finn* reveals Tom to be even more callous and manipulative than we realized. The bullet in Tom's leg seems rather deserved when Tom reveals that he has known all along that Miss Watson has been dead for two months and that she freed Jim in her will. Tom's confession reveals a new depth of cruelty: he treats blacks only a little better than slaveholders do, using Jim as a plaything to indulge in a great "adventure." Tom's claim that he meant to pay Jim for his troubles is surely of little consolation to anyone, and indeed, the very idea of making up for such callousness with money is deeply insulting. However, no one ever chastises Tom for his behavior. Instead, he turns the bullet—the symbol of the fine line between fun and foolishness—into a trophy, and he proposes to Huck that they go look for more adventures among the "Injuns," another people ravaged and oppressed by whites.

At the end of the novel, Tom seems to be beyond reform, Huck opts out of society in his desire to go to Oklahoma, and the other adults are left in compromised positions. Jim is the only character who comes out of the mess looking like a respectable adult. By helping the doctor treat Tom and shielding Huck from seeing his father's corpse, Jim yet again affirms that he is a decent human being. The Phelpses, although they immediately try to make amends for their previous treatment of Jim, still own slaves. Miss Watson, although she has done the right thing by freeing Jim, sullies her good intentions by making the action a provision of her will, something to be carried out in the future—at her death—rather than immediately. Aunt Sally smothers, Aunt Polly scolds, and everyone bumbles along. In the end, it is no wonder Huck wants to avoid further "sivilizing."

Possibly the most troubling aspect of the novel's close is the realization that all has been for naught. Jim has, technically, been a free man almost the entire time. All of Huck's moral crises, all the lies he has told, all the societal conventions he has broken, have been part of a great game. In a way, the knowledge of Jim's emancipation erases the novel that has come before it. Ultimately, we are left questioning the meaning of what we have read: perhaps Twain means the novel as a reminder that life is ultimately a matter of imperfect information and ambiguous situations, and that the best one can do is to follow one's head and heart. Perhaps Twain, finishing this novel twenty years after the Civil War concluded and slaves were freed, means also to say that black Americans may be free in a technical sense, but that they remain chained by a society that refuses to acknowledge their rightful and equal standing as individuals. In a sense, perhaps Tom's mistreatment of Jim is actually a boon, for it leads the other characters in the novel to acknowledge Jim as a worthy human being. In the end, *Huckleberry Finn* moves beyond questions of slavery, to broader questions of morality and race. Unfortunately, these questions seldom have straightforward answers, and thus the ending of the novel contains as many new problems as solutions.

IMPORTANT QUOTATIONS EXPLAINED

1. The Widow Douglas she took me for her son, and allowed
    she would sivilize me; but it was rough living in the house
    all the time, considering how dismal regular and decent
    the widow was in all her ways; and so when I couldn't
    stand it no longer I lit out. I got into my old rags and my
    sugar-hogshead again, and was free and satisfied. But Tom
    Sawyer he hunted me up and said he was going to start a
    band of robbers, and I might join if I would go back to the
    widow and be respectable. So I went back.

In these lines, which appear on the first page of the novel, Huck
discusses events that have occurred since the end of *The Adventures
of Tom Sawyer,* the novel in which he made his first appearance.
Here, Huck establishes his opposition to "sivilizing," which seems
natural for a thirteen-year-old boy rebelling against his parents
and other authorities. Our initial inclination may be to laugh and
dismiss Huck's urges for freedom. At the same time, however, we
see that Huck's problems with civilized society are based on some
rather mature observations about the worth of that society. Huck
goes on to associate civilization and respectability with a childish
game—Tom's band of robbers, in which the participants are to pretend to be criminals. Under the influence of his friend, Huck gives
in and returns to the Widow's, but as the novel progresses, his dis-
like for society reappears and influences the important decisions he
makes.

2.   I hadn't had a bite to eat since yesterday, so Jim he got out
      some corn-dodgers and buttermilk, and pork and cabbage
      and greens—there ain't nothing in the world so good when
      it's cooked right—and whilst I eat my supper we talked
      and had a good time. . . .We said there warn't no home like
      a raft, after all. Other places do seem so cramped up and
      smothery, but a raft don't. You feel mighty free and easy
      and comfortable on a raft.

At this point in Chapter XVIII, Huck has just escaped from the
Grangerford-Shepherdson feud and is thoroughly sickened by society. Compared to the outrageous incidents onshore, the raft represents a retreat from the outside world, the site of simple pleasures
and good companionship. Even the simple food Jim offers Huck
is delicious in this atmosphere of freedom and comfort. Huck and
Jim do not have to answer to anyone on the raft, and it represents a
kind of utopian life for them. They try to maintain this idyllic separation from society and its problems, but as the raft makes its way
southward, unsavory influences from onshore repeatedly invade the
world of the raft. In a sense, Twain's portrayal of life on the raft and
the river is a romantic one, but tempered by the realistic knowledge
that the evils and problems of the world are inescapable.

QUOTATIONS

3. It was a close place. I took . . . up [the letter I'd written to Miss Watson], and held it in my hand. I was a-trembling, because I'd got to decide, forever, betwixt two things, and I knowed it. I studied a minute, sort of holding my breath, and then says to myself: "All right then, I'll go to hell"— and tore it up. It was awful thoughts and awful words, but they was said. And I let them stay said; and never thought no more about reforming.

These lines from Chapter XXXI describe the moral climax of the novel. The duke and the dauphin have sold Jim, who is being held in the Phelpses' shed pending his return to his rightful owner. Thinking that life at home in St. Petersburg—even if it means Jim will still be a slave and Huck will be a captive of the Widow— would be better than his current state of peril far from home, Huck composes a letter to Miss Watson, telling her where Jim is. When Huck thinks of his friendship with Jim, however, and realizes that Jim will be sold down the river anyway, he decides to tear up the letter. The logical consequences of Huck's action, rather than the lessons society has taught him, drive Huck. He decides that going to "hell," if it means following his gut and not society's hypocritical and cruel principles, is a better option than going to everyone else's heaven. This moment of decision represents Huck's true break with the world around him. At this point, Huck decides to help Jim escape slavery once and for all. Huck also realizes that he does not want to reenter the "sivilized" world: after all his experiences and moral development on the river, he wants to move on to the freedom of the West instead.

QUOTATIONS

4. Tom told me what his plan was, and I see in a minute it was worth fifteen of mine for style, and would make Jim just as free a man as mine would, and maybe get us all killed besides. So I was satisfied, and said we would waltz in on it.

In this quotation from Chapter XXXIV, we see Huck once again swayed by his friend Tom. Although in practical terms it would be quite simple to break Jim out of the shed, Tom insists on a more complicated plan with "style." Dependent on Tom not to blow his cover—at this point, Huck is pretending, for the benefit of the Phelpses, to be Tom, while Tom is pretending to be his brother Sid—Huck has to go along. Indeed, as we see, Tom's return in the final chapters of the novel temporarily stops or reverses Huck's development: Huck, in many ways, reverts to the status of Tom's follower that he occupied at the beginning of the novel. Nonetheless, Huck maintains his characteristic realistic outlook on the world, and his prediction that Tom's plan could get them killed is more accurate than he knows.

QUOTATIONS

5. But I reckon I got to light out for the territory ahead of the rest, because Aunt Sally she's going to adopt me and sivilize me, and I can't stand it. I been there before.

These lines are the last in the novel. By the final chapter, most everything has been resolved: Jim is free, Tom is on his way to recovering from a bullet wound, and Aunt Sally has offered to adopt Huck. Although Huck has come to like Sally and Silas, he knows they are still a part of the society he has come to distrust and fear. Aunt Sally's intentions for Huck center around the upbringing that society thinks every boy should have: religion, clean clothes, education, and an indoctrination in right and wrong. Huck, however, has come to realize that the first two are useless and that, in reference to the third, he can provide a much better version for himself than can society. The "territories," the relatively unsettled western United States, will offer Huck an opportunity to be himself, in a world not yet "sivilized" and thus brimming with promise. Weary of his old life, Huck contemplates ways to continue living with the same freedom he felt on the raft. Huck's break from society is complete, and before the dust from his adventures is fully settled, he is already scheming to detach himself again.

QUOTATIONS

KEY FACTS

FULL TITLE
The Adventures of Huckleberry Finn

AUTHOR
Mark Twain (pseudonym for Samuel Clemens)

TYPE OF WORK
Novel

GENRE
Picaresque novel (episodic, colorful story often in the form
of a quest or journey); satire of popular adventure and
romance novels; bildungsroman (novel of education or moral
development)

LANGUAGE
English; frequently makes use of Southern and black dialects of
the time

TIME AND PLACE WRITTEN
1876–1883; Hartford, Connecticut, and Elmira, New York

DATE OF FIRST PUBLICATION
1884

PUBLISHER
Charles L. Webster & Co.

NARRATOR
Huckleberry Finn

POINT OF VIEW
Huck's point of view, although Twain occasionally indulges in
digressions in which he shows off his own ironic wit

TONE
Frequently ironic or mocking, particularly concerning
adventure novels and romances; also contemplative, as
Huck seeks to decipher the world around him; sometimes
boyish and exuberant

TENSE
> Immediate past

SETTING (TIME)
> Before the Civil War; roughly 1835–1845; Twain said the novel was set forty to fifty years before the time of its publication

SETTING (PLACE)
> The Mississippi River town of St. Petersburg, Missouri; various locations along the river through Arkansas

PROTAGONIST
> Huck Finn

MAJOR CONFLICT
> At the beginning of the novel, Huck struggles against society and its attempts to civilize him, represented by the Widow Douglas, Miss Watson, and other adults. Later, this conflict gains greater focus in Huck's dealings with Jim, as Huck must decide whether to turn Jim in, as society demands, or to protect and help his friend instead.

RISING ACTION
> Miss Watson and the Widow Douglas attempt to civilize Huck until Pap reappears in town, demands Huck's money, and kidnaps Huck. Huck escapes society by faking his own death and retreating to Jackson's Island, where he meets Jim and sets out on the river with him. Huck gradually begins to question the rules society has taught him, as when, in order to protect Jim, he lies and makes up a story to scare off some men searching for escaped slaves. Although Huck and Jim live a relatively peaceful life on the raft, they are ultimately unable to escape the evils and hypocrisies of the outside world. The most notable representatives of these outside evils are the con men the duke and the dauphin, who engage in a series of increasingly serious scams that culminate in their sale of Jim, who ends up at the Phelps farm.

CLIMAX
> Huck considers but then decides against writing Miss Watson to tell her the Phelps family is holding Jim, following his conscience rather than the prevailing morality of the day. Instead, Tom and Huck try to free Jim, and Tom is shot in the leg during the attempt.

FALLING ACTION

When Aunt Polly arrives at the Phelps farm and correctly identifies Tom and Huck, Tom reveals that Miss Watson died two months earlier and freed Jim in her will. Afterward, Tom recovers from his wound, while Huck decides he is done with civilized society and makes plans to travel to the West.

THEMES

Racism and slavery; intellectual and moral education; the hypocrisy of "civilized" society

MOTIFS

Childhood; lies and cons; superstitions and folk beliefs; parodies of popular romance novels

SYMBOLS

The Mississippi River; floods; shipwrecks; the natural world

FORESHADOWING

Twain uses parallels and juxtapositions more so than explicit foreshadowing, especially in his frequent comparisons between Huck's plight and eventual escape and Jim's plight and eventual escape.

KEY FACTS

STUDY QUESTIONS

1. *Huck Finn is a thirteen-year-old boy. Why does Twain use a child as the center of consciousness in this book?*

In using a child protagonist, Twain is able to imply a comparison between the powerlessness and vulnerability of a child and the powerlessness and vulnerability of a black man in pre–Civil War America. Huck and Jim frequently find themselves in the same predicaments: each is abused, each faces the threat of losing his freedom, and each is constantly at the mercy of adult white men. As we see in Huck's moral dilemmas, however, Jim is also vulnerable to Huck, who, although he occupies the lowest rung of the white social ladder, is white nonetheless. Twain also uses his child protagonist to dramatize the conflict between societal or received morality on the one hand and a different kind of morality based on intuition and experience on the other. As a boy, Huck is a character who can develop morally, whose mind is still open and being formed, who does not take his principles and values for granted. By tracing the education and experiences of a boy, Twain shows that conclusions about right and wrong that are based on logic and experience often stand at odds with the society's rules and morals, which are often hypocritical rather than logical.

2. *Discuss Twain's use of dialects in the novel. What effect does this usage have on the reader? Does it make the novel less of an artistic achievement?*

Twain's use of dialect, which has proved controversial over the years, lends to the overall realism and vividness of *Huckleberry Finn*. Because it is sometimes difficult to decipher the character's speech while reading, we are almost forced to read aloud: at the very least, to read this novel, one has to be able to "hear" the voices in one's own head. Performance is important in this novel, as Tom Sawyer's follies and the duke and the dauphin's cons demonstrate. Furthermore, in the world of the novel, the way in which a character speaks is closely tied to that character's status in society. Huck, who was born in poverty and has lived on the margins of society ever since, speaks in a much rougher, more uneducated-sounding dialect than the speech Tom uses. Jim's speech, meanwhile, which seems rough and uneducated, is frequently not all that different from Huck's speech or the speech of other white characters. In this way, Twain implies that it is society, wealth, and upbringing, rather than any sort of innate ignorance or roughness, that determines an individual's educational opportunities and manner of self-expression.

3. *Discuss the use of the river as a symbol in the novel.*

At the beginning of *The Adventures of Huckleberry Finn*, the river is a symbol of freedom and change. Huck and Jim flow with the water and never remain in one place long enough to be pinned down by a particular set of rules. Compared to the "civilized" towns along the banks of the Mississippi, the raft on the river represents an peaceful, alternative space where Huck and Jim, free of hassles and disapproving stares, can enjoy one another's company and revel in the small pleasures of life, like smoking a pipe and watching the stars.

As the novel continues, however, the real world beyond the Mississippi's banks quickly intrudes on the calm, protected space of the river. Huck and Jim come across wrecks and threatening snags, and bounty hunters, thieves, and con artists accost them. Although the river still provides refuge when things go wrong ashore, Huck and Jim's relation to the river seems to change and become less friendly. After they miss the mouth of the Ohio River, the Mississippi ceases to carry them toward freedom. Instead, the current sweeps them toward the Deep South, which represents the ultimate threat to Jim and a dead end for Huck. Just as the Mississippi would inevitably carry Huck and Jim to New Orleans (where Miss Watson had wanted to send Jim anyway), escape from the evils inherent in humanity is never truly possible.

How to Write
Literary Analysis

The Literary Essay: A Step-by-Step Guide

When you read for pleasure, your only goal is enjoyment. You might find yourself reading to get caught up in an exciting story, to learn about an interesting time or place, or just to pass time. Maybe you're looking for inspiration, guidance, or a reflection of your own life. There are as many different, valid ways of reading a book as there are books in the world.

When you read a work of literature in an English class, however, you're being asked to read in a special way: you're being asked to perform *literary analysis*. To analyze something means to break it down into smaller parts and then examine how those parts work, both individually and together. Literary analysis involves examining all the parts of a novel, play, short story, or poem—elements such as character, setting, tone, and imagery—and thinking about how the author uses those elements to create certain effects.

A literary essay isn't a book review: you're not being asked whether or not you liked a book or whether you'd recommend it to another reader. A literary essay also isn't like the kind of book report you wrote when you were younger, where your teacher wanted you to summarize the book's action. A high school- or college-level literary essay asks, "How does this piece of literature actually work?" "How does it do what it does?" and, "Why might the author have made the choices he or she did?"

The Seven Steps
No one is born knowing how to analyze literature; it's a skill you learn and a process you can master. As you gain more practice with this kind of thinking and writing, you'll be able to craft a method that works best for you. But until then, here are seven basic steps to writing a well-constructed literary essay:

1. Ask questions
2. Collect evidence
3. Construct a thesis

68

4. Develop and organize arguments
5. Write the introduction
6. Write the body paragraphs
7. Write the conclusion

---

1. Ask Questions

When you're assigned a literary essay in class, your teacher will often provide you with a list of writing prompts. Lucky you! Now all you have to do is choose one. Do yourself a favor and pick a topic that interests you. You'll have a much better (not to mention easier) time if you start off with something you enjoy thinking about. If you are asked to come up with a topic by yourself, though, you might start to feel a little panicked. Maybe you have too many ideas—or none at all. Don't worry. Take a deep breath and start by asking yourself these questions:

- **What struck you?** Did a particular image, line, or scene linger in your mind for a long time? If it fascinated you, chances are you can draw on it to write a fascinating essay.

- **What confused you?** Maybe you were surprised to see a character act in a certain way, or maybe you didn't understand why the book ended the way it did. Confusing moments in a work of literature are like a loose thread in a sweater: if you pull on it, you can unravel the entire thing. Ask yourself why the author chose to write about that character or scene the way he or she did and you might tap into some important insights about the work as a whole.

- **Did you notice any patterns?** Is there a phrase that the main character uses constantly or an image that repeats throughout the book? If you can figure out how that pattern weaves through the work and what the significance of that pattern is, you've almost got your entire essay mapped out.

- **Did you notice any contradictions or ironies?** Great works of literature are complex; great literary essays recognize and explain those complexities. Maybe the title (*Happy Days*) totally disagrees with the book's subject matter (hungry orphans dying in the woods). Maybe the main character acts one way around his family and a completely different way around his friends and associates. If you can find a way to explain a work's contradictory elements, you've got the seeds of a great essay.

At this point, you don't need to know exactly what you're going to say about your topic; you just need a place to begin your exploration. You can help direct your reading and brainstorming by formulating your topic as a *question,* which you'll then try to answer in your essay. The best questions invite critical debates and discussions, not just a rehashing of the summary. Remember, you're looking for something you can *prove or argue* based on evidence you find in the text. Finally, remember to keep the scope of your question in mind: is this a topic you can adequately address within the word or page limit you've been given? Conversely, is this a topic big enough to fill the required length?

GOOD QUESTIONS

> *"Are Romeo and Juliet's parents responsible for the deaths of their children?"*
>> *"Why do pigs keep showing up in* LORD OF THE FLIES*?"*
>> *"Are Dr. Frankenstein and his monster alike? How?"*

BAD QUESTIONS

>> *"What happens to Scout in* TO KILL A MOCKINGBIRD*?"*
>> *"What do the other characters in* JULIUS CAESAR *think about Caesar?"*
>> *"How does Hester Prynne in* THE SCARLET LETTER *remind me of my sister?"*

---

2. COLLECT EVIDENCE

Once you know what question you want to answer, it's time to scour the book for things that will help you answer the question. Don't worry if you don't know what you want to say yet—right now you're just collecting ideas and material and letting it all percolate. Keep track of passages, symbols, images, or scenes that deal with your topic. Eventually, you'll start making connections between these examples and your thesis will emerge.

Here's a brief summary of the various parts that compose each and every work of literature. These are the elements that you will analyze in your essay, and which you will offer as evidence to support your arguments. For more on the parts of literary works, see the Glossary of Literary Terms at the end of this section.

LITERARY ANALYSIS

ELEMENTS OF STORY   These are the *what*s of the work—what happens, where it happens, and to whom it happens.

- **Plot:** All of the events and actions of the work.

- **Character:** The people who act and are acted upon in a literary work. The main character of a work is known as the *protagonist.*

- **Conflict:** The central tension in the work. In most cases, the protagonist wants something, while opposing forces (antagonists) hinder the protagonist's progress.

- **Setting:** When and where the work takes place. Elements of setting include location, time period, time of day, weather, social atmosphere, and economic conditions.

- **Narrator:** The person telling the story. The narrator may straightforwardly report what happens, convey the subjective opinions and perceptions of one or more characters, or provide commentary and opinion in his or her own voice.

- **Themes:** The main idea or message of the work—usually an abstract idea about people, society, or life in general. A work may have many themes, which may be in tension with one another.

ELEMENTS OF STYLE   These are the *how*s—how the characters speak, how the story is constructed, and how language is used throughout the work.

- **Structure and organization:** How the parts of the work are assembled. Some novels are narrated in a linear, chronological fashion, while others skip around in time. Some plays follow a traditional three- or five-act structure, while others are a series of loosely connected scenes. Some authors deliberately leave gaps in their works, leaving readers to puzzle out the missing information. A work's structure and organization can tell you a lot about the kind of message it wants to convey.

- **Point of view:** The perspective from which a story is told. In *first-person point of view,* the narrator involves him or herself in the story. ("I went to the store"; "We watched in horror as the bird slammed into the window.") A first-person narrator is usually the protagonist of the work, but not always. In *third-person point of view,* the narrator does not participate in the story. A third-person narrator may closely follow a specific character, recounting that individual character's thoughts or experiences, or it may be what we call an *omniscient* narrator. Omniscient narrators see and know all: they can witness any event in any time or place and are privy to the inner thoughts and feelings of all characters. Remember that the narrator and the author are not the same thing!

- **Diction:** Word choice. Whether a character uses dry, clinical language or flowery prose with lots of exclamation points can tell you a lot about his or her attitude and personality.

- **Syntax:** Word order and sentence construction. Syntax is a crucial part of establishing an author's narrative voice. Ernest Hemingway, for example, is known for writing in very short, straightforward sentences, while James Joyce characteristically wrote in long, incredibly complicated lines.

- **Tone:** The mood or feeling of the text. Diction and syntax often contribute to the tone of a work. A novel written in short, clipped sentences that use small, simple words might feel brusque, cold, or matter-of-fact.

- **Imagery:** Language that appeals to the senses, representing things that can be seen, smelled, heard, tasted, or touched.

- **Figurative language:** Language that is not meant to be interpreted literally. The most common types of figurative language are *metaphors* and *similes,* which compare two unlike things in order to suggest a similarity between them— for example, "All the world's a stage," or "The moon is like a ball of green cheese." (Metaphors say one thing *is* another thing; similes claim that one thing is *like* another thing.)

---

3. CONSTRUCT A THESIS

When you've examined all the evidence you've collected and know how you want to answer the question, it's time to write your thesis statement. A *thesis* is a claim about a work of literature that needs to be supported by evidence and arguments. The thesis statement is the heart of the literary essay, and the bulk of your paper will be spent trying to prove this claim. A good thesis will be:

- **Arguable.** "*The Great Gatsby* describes New York society in the 1920s" isn't a thesis—it's a fact.

- **Provable through textual evidence.** "*Hamlet* is a confusing but ultimately very well-written play" is a weak thesis because it offers the writer's personal opinion about the book. Yes, it's arguable, but it's not a claim that can be proved or supported with examples taken from the play itself.

- **Surprising.** "Both George and Lenny change a great deal in *Of Mice and Men*" is a weak thesis because it's obvious. A really strong thesis will argue for a reading of the text that is not immediately apparent.

- **Specific.** "Dr. Frankenstein's monster tells us a lot about the human condition" is *almost* a really great thesis statement, but it's still too vague. What does the writer mean by "a lot"? *How* does the monster tell us so much about the human condition?

GOOD THESIS STATEMENTS

Question: In *Romeo and Juliet*, which is more powerful in shaping the lovers' story: fate or foolishness?

Thesis: "Though Shakespeare defines Romeo and Juliet as 'star-crossed lovers' and images of stars and planets appear throughout the play, a closer examination of that celestial imagery reveals that the stars are merely witnesses to the characters' foolish activities and not the causes themselves."

Question: How does the bell jar function as a symbol in Sylvia Plath's *The Bell Jar*?

Thesis: "A bell jar is a bell-shaped glass that has three basic uses: to hold a specimen for observation, to contain gases, and to maintain a vacuum. The bell jar appears in each of these capacities in *The Bell Jar*, Plath's semi-autobiographical novel, and each appearance marks a different stage in Esther's mental breakdown."

Question: Would Piggy in *The Lord of the Flies* make a good island leader if he were given the chance?

Thesis: "Though the intelligent, rational, and innovative Piggy has the mental characteristics of a good leader, he ultimately lacks the social skills necessary to be an effective one. Golding emphasizes this point by giving Piggy a foil in the charismatic Jack, whose magnetic personality allows him to capture and wield power effectively, if not always wisely."

4. DEVELOP AND ORGANIZE ARGUMENTS

The reasons and examples that support your thesis will form the middle paragraphs of your essay. Since you can't really write your thesis statement until you know how you'll structure your argument, you'll probably end up working on steps 3 and 4 at the same time.

There's no single method of argumentation that will work in every context. One essay prompt might ask you to compare and contrast two characters, while another asks you to trace an image through a given work of literature. These questions require different kinds of answers and therefore different kinds of arguments. Below, we'll discuss three common kinds of essay prompts and some strategies for constructing a solid, well-argued case.

TYPES OF LITERARY ESSAYS

- **Compare and contrast**

    Compare and contrast the characters of Huck and Jim in THE ADVENTURES OF HUCKLEBERRY FINN.

    Chances are you've written this kind of essay before. In an academic literary context, you'll organize your arguments the same way you would in any other class. You can either go *subject by subject* or *point by point*. In the former, you'll discuss one character first and then the second. In the latter, you'll choose several traits (attitude toward life, social status, images and metaphors associated with the character) and devote a paragraph to each. You may want to use a mix of these two approaches—for example, you may want to spend a paragraph a piece broadly sketching Huck's and Jim's personalities before transitioning into a paragraph or two that describes a few key points of comparison. This can be a highly effective strategy if you want to make a counterintuitive argument—that, despite seeming to be totally different, the two objects being compared are actually similar in a very important way (or vice versa). Remember that your essay should reveal something fresh or unexpected about the text, so think beyond the obvious parallels and differences.

- **Trace**

    Choose an image—for example, birds, knives, or eyes—and trace that image throughout MACBETH.

    Sounds pretty easy, right? All you need to do is read the play, underline every appearance of a knife in *Macbeth,* and then list them in your essay in the order they appear, right? Well, not exactly. Your teacher doesn't want a simple catalog of examples. He or she wants to see you make *connections* between those examples—that's the difference between summarizing and analyzing. In the *Macbeth* example above, think about the different contexts in which knives appear in the play and to what effect. In *Macbeth*, there are real knives and imagined knives; knives that kill and knives that simply threaten. Categorize and classify your examples to give them some order. Finally, always keep the overall effect in mind. After you choose and analyze your examples, you should come to some greater understanding about the work, as well as your chosen image, symbol, or phrase's role in developing the major themes and stylistic strategies of that work.

- **Debate**

  Is the society depicted in 1984 good for its citizens?

  In this kind of essay, you're being asked to debate a moral, ethical, or aesthetic issue regarding the work. You might be asked to judge a character or group of characters (*Is Caesar responsible for his own demise?*) or the work itself (*Is* JANE EYRE *a feminist novel?*). For this kind of essay, there are two important points to keep in mind. First, don't simply base your arguments on your personal feelings and reactions. Every literary essay expects you to read and analyze the work, so search for evidence in the text. What do characters in *1984* have to say about the government of Oceania? What images does Orwell use that might give you a hint about his attitude toward the government? As in any debate, you also need to make sure that you define all the necessary terms before you begin to argue your case. What does it mean to be a "good" society? What makes a novel "feminist"? You should define your terms right up front, in the first paragraph after your introduction.

  Second, remember that strong literary essays make contrary and surprising arguments. Try to think outside the box. In the *1984* example above, it seems like the obvious answer would be no, the totalitarian society depicted in Orwell's novel is *not* good for its citizens. But can you think of any arguments for the opposite side? Even if your final assertion is that the novel depicts a cruel, repressive, and therefore harmful society, acknowledging and responding to the counterargument will strengthen your overall case.

5. WRITE THE INTRODUCTION

Your introduction sets up the entire essay. It's where you present your topic and articulate the particular issues and questions you'll be addressing. It's also where you, as the writer, introduce yourself to your readers. A persuasive literary essay immediately establishes its writer as a knowledgeable, authoritative figure.

An introduction can vary in length depending on the overall length of the essay, but in a traditional five-paragraph essay it should be no longer than one paragraph. However long it is, your introduction needs to:

- **Provide any necessary context.** Your introduction should situate the reader and let him or her know what to expect. What book are you discussing? Which characters? What topic will you be addressing?

- **Answer the "So what?" question.** Why is this topic important, and why is your particular position on the topic noteworthy? Ideally, your introduction should pique the reader's interest by suggesting how your argument is surprising or otherwise counterintuitive. Literary essays make unexpected connections and reveal less-than-obvious truths.

- **Present your thesis.** This usually happens at or very near the end of your introduction.

- **Indicate the shape of the essay to come.** Your reader should finish reading your introduction with a good sense of the scope of your essay as well as the path you'll take toward proving your thesis. You don't need to spell out every step, but you do need to suggest the organizational pattern you'll be using.

Your introduction should not:

- **Be vague.** Beware of the two killer words in literary analysis: *interesting* and *important*. Of course the work, question, or example is interesting and important—that's why you're writing about it!

- **Open with any grandiose assertions.** Many student readers think that beginning their essays with a flamboyant statement such as, "Since the dawn of time, writers have been fascinated with the topic of free will," makes them

sound important and commanding. You know what? It
actually sounds pretty amateurish.

- **Wildly praise the work.** Another typical mistake student
  writers make is extolling the work or author. Your teacher
  doesn't need to be told that "Shakespeare is perhaps the
  greatest writer in the English language." You can mention
  a work's reputation in passing—by referring to *The Adventures of Huckleberry Finn* as "Mark Twain's enduring
  classic," for example—but don't make a point of bringing it
  up unless that reputation is key to your argument.

- **Go off-topic.** Keep your introduction streamlined and to
  the point. Don't feel the need to throw in all kinds of bells
  and whistles in order to impress your reader—just get to the
  point as quickly as you can, without skimping on any of the
  required steps.

---

6. Write the Body Paragraphs

Once you've written your introduction, you'll take the arguments
you developed in step 4 and turn them into your body paragraphs.
The organization of this middle section of your essay will largely be
determined by the argumentative strategy you use, but no matter
how you arrange your thoughts, your body paragraphs need to do
the following:

- **Begin with a strong topic sentence.** Topic sentences are like
  signs on a highway: they tell the reader where they are and
  where they're going. A good topic sentence not only alerts
  readers to what issue will be discussed in the following
  paragraph but also gives them a sense of what argument
  will be made *about* that issue. "Rumor and gossip play an
  important role in *The Crucible*" isn't a strong topic sentence
  because it doesn't tell us very much. "The community's
  constant gossiping creates an environment that allows false
  accusations to flourish" is a much stronger topic sentence—
  it not only tells us *what* the paragraph will discuss (gossip)
  but *how* the paragraph will discuss the topic (by showing
  how gossip creates a set of conditions that leads to the play's
  climactic action).

- **Fully and completely develop a single thought.** Don't skip
  around in your paragraph or try to stuff in too much
  material. Body paragraphs are like bricks: each individual

one needs to be strong and sturdy or the entire structure will collapse. Make sure you have really proven your point before moving on to the next one.

- **Use transitions effectively.** Good literary essay writers know that each paragraph must be clearly and strongly linked to the material around it. Think of each paragraph as a response to the one that precedes it. Use transition words and phrases such as *however, similarly, on the contrary, therefore,* and *furthermore* to indicate what kind of response you're making.

---

7. WRITE THE CONCLUSION

Just as you used the introduction to ground your readers in the topic before providing your thesis, you'll use the conclusion to quickly summarize the specifics learned thus far and then hint at the broader implications of your topic. A good conclusion will:

- **Do more than simply restate the thesis.** If your thesis argued that *The Catcher in the Rye* can be read as a Christian allegory, don't simply end your essay by saying, "And that is why *The Catcher in the Rye* can be read as a Christian allegory." If you've constructed your arguments well, this kind of statement will just be redundant.

- **Synthesize the arguments, not summarize them.** Similarly, don't repeat the details of your body paragraphs in your conclusion. The reader has already read your essay, and chances are it's not so long that they've forgotten all your points by now.

- **Revisit the "So what?" question.** In your introduction, you made a case for why your topic and position are important. You should close your essay with the same sort of gesture. What do your readers know now that they didn't know before? How will that knowledge help them better appreciate or understand the work overall?

- **Move from the specific to the general.** Your essay has most likely treated a very specific element of the work—a single character, a small set of images, or a particular passage. In your conclusion, try to show how this narrow discussion has wider implications for the work overall. If your essay on *To Kill a Mockingbird* focused on the character of Boo Radley, for example, you might want to include a bit in your conclusion about how he fits into the novel's larger message about childhood, innocence, or family life.

- **Stay relevant.** Your conclusion should suggest new directions of thought, but it shouldn't be treated as an opportunity to pad your essay with all the extra, interesting ideas you came up with during your brainstorming sessions but couldn't fit into the essay proper. Don't attempt to stuff in unrelated queries or too many abstract thoughts.

- **Avoid making overblown closing statements.** A conclusion should open up your highly specific, focused discussion, but it should do so without drawing a sweeping lesson about life or human nature. Making such observations may be part of the point of reading, but it's almost always a mistake in essays, where these observations tend to sound overly dramatic or simply silly.

A+ Essay Checklist

Congratulations! If you've followed all the steps we've outlined above, you should have a solid literary essay to show for all your efforts. What if you've got your sights set on an A+? To write the kind of superlative essay that will be rewarded with a perfect grade, keep the following rubric in mind. These are the qualities that teachers expect to see in a truly A+ essay. How does yours stack up?

✓ Demonstrates a thorough understanding of the book
✓ Presents an original, compelling argument
✓ Thoughtfully analyzes the text's formal elements
✓ Uses appropriate and insightful examples
✓ Structures ideas in a logical and progressive order
✓ Demonstrates a mastery of sentence construction, transitions, grammar, spelling, and word choice

LITERARY ANALYSIS

SUGGESTED ESSAY TOPICS

1. *Lying occurs frequently in this novel. Curiously, some lies, like those Huck tells to save Jim, seem to be "good" lies, while others, like the cons of the duke and the dauphin, seem to be "bad." What is the difference? Are both "wrong"? Why does so much lying go on in* HUCKLEBERRY FINN?

2. *Describe some of the models for families that appear in the novel. What is the importance of family structures? What is their place in society? Do Huck and Jim constitute a family? What about Huck and Tom? When does society intervene in the family?*

3. *The revelation at the novel's end that Tom has known all along that Jim is a free man is startling. Is Tom inexcusably cruel? Or is he just being a normal thirteen-year-old boy? Does Tom's behavior comment on society in some larger way?*

4. *What techniques does Twain use to create sympathy for his characters, in particular, Jim? Are these techniques effective?*

5. *Discuss the place of morality in* HUCKLEBERRY FINN. *In the world of the novel, where do moral values come from? The community? The family? The church? One's experiences? Which of these potential sources does Twain privilege over the others? Which does he mock, or describe disapprovingly?*

6. *Why might Twain have decided to set the novel in a time before the abolition of slavery, despite the fact that he published it in 1885, two decades after the end of the Civil War?*

A+ Student Essay

Do Huck and Jim forge a friendship that transcends the
limits of race? Or do race and racism prove inescapable?

Much of the scholarly criticism written on Mark Twain's masterpiece *Huckleberry Finn* analyzes the novel's depiction of and attitude toward race and racism. Over the years, readers have asked
whether Huckleberry Finn is a racist boy or a smart kid eager to
interrogate the bigoted beliefs of white society; whether Twain portrays Jim as a three-dimensional human or as a collection of stereotypes; and to what degree Twain himself shared the racist views he
parodies in his novel. While *Huckleberry Finn* is a novel obsessed
with race, however, it is also a novel obsessed with the absence of
race. Huck and Jim find happiness only on Jackson's Island, the site
of their first meeting, where the two manage to briefly transcend
race altogether. Because of their unusual circumstances, Huck and
Jim momentarily turn their white boy/black slave identities upside
down, an achievement Twain portrays as deeply desirable.

Huck and Jim are uniquely suited to the blurring of race and
identity that occurs on Jackson's Island. Both are intelligent, despite
their lack of formal education; both question conventional wisdom
and view events from a skewed angle; and both are good at heart
and tend to empathize with people, including those who are unlike
themselves. In addition, both are outsiders in society. As a slave,
Jim is viewed as less than human by whites. While Huck is infinitely
more privileged because of his whiteness, he is nonetheless an out-
lier due to his poverty, his drunken, violent father, and his frequent
homelessness. Because of their smarts, their inquisitiveness, their
compassion, and their mutual alienation from society, Huck and
Jim are far less likely than other characters in the novel to view race
as a rigid mold into which people are poured at birth.

On Jackson's Island, Huck and Jim achieve a kind of racelessness.
Here, they don't act like an escaped slave and a white kid on the lam;
they act like partners, helping each other and, as Jim does for Huck,
forgiving each other. Their identities become fluid. In Chapter IX,
Jim becomes a father figure to Huck, reversing the traditional slave-
master relationship. Jim conceals the shocking sight of Pap's corpse
from Huck, a gesture that conveys Jim's protective paternal qualities
and suggests that, though Huck has lost his biological father, he has

gained a spiritual one. In this moment, Pap's role transfers to Jim, and Jim steps into the shoes of a middle-aged white man. Later, in Chapter X, Huck takes on the identity of a girl, donning a dress and practicing a feminine shtick. These wild reversals suggest that on the island, identities are turned on their heads. There is no doubt that Twain heartily condones this topsy-turviness. He portrays Jackson's Island as an Eden, a glorious refuge where food abounds. Anything that happens there, he suggests, is desirable and good.

The charmed time cannot last long, however. Almost before it has begun, it ends, and Jim and Huck find themselves back in their familiar, polarized, black-and-white world, where kind women speak cheerfully about hunting down escaped slaves and Huck feels guilty about his failure to turn in Jim, Miss Watson's "stolen property." Their identities continue to slip and shift throughout the novel; after all, simply by traveling together and relying on each other, Huck and Jim blur the racial boundaries between them. But the realities of race weigh heavily on them after they leave Jackson's Island. The extreme brevity of their raceless idyll suggests that it is nearly impossible to create a society that doesn't classify people according to the color of their skin. But the fact that the idyll exists at all, even for a moment, demonstrates Twain's fundamental optimism about the future of race relations in America.

Glossary of Literary Terms

ANTAGONIST

The entity that acts to frustrate the goals of the *protagonist*. The antagonist is usually another *character* but may also be a non-human force.

ANTIHERO / ANTIHEROINE

A *protagonist* who is not admirable or who challenges notions of what should be considered admirable.

CHARACTER

A person, animal, or any other thing with a personality that appears in a *narrative*.

CLIMAX

The moment of greatest intensity in a text or the major turning point in the *plot*.

CONFLICT

The central struggle that moves the *plot* forward. The conflict can be the *protagonist*'s struggle against fate, nature, society, or another person.

FIRST-PERSON POINT OF VIEW

A literary style in which the *narrator* tells the story from his or her own *point of view* and refers to himself or herself as "I." The narrator may be an active participant in the story or just an observer.

HERO / HEROINE

The principal *character* in a literary work or *narrative*.

IMAGERY

Language that brings to mind sense-impressions, representing things that can be seen, smelled, heard, tasted, or touched.

MOTIF

A recurring idea, structure, contrast, or device that develops or informs the major *themes* of a work of literature.

NARRATIVE

A story.

NARRATOR

The person (sometimes a *character*) who tells a story; the *voice* assumed by the writer. The narrator and the author of the work of literature are not the same person.

PLOT

The arrangement of the events in a story, including the sequence in which they are told, the relative emphasis they are given, and the causal connections between events.

POINT OF VIEW

The *perspective* that a *narrative* takes toward the events it describes.

PROTAGONIST

The main *character* around whom the story revolves.

SETTING

The location of a *narrative* in time and space. Setting creates mood or atmosphere.

SUBPLOT

A secondary *plot* that is of less importance to the overall story but may serve as a point of contrast or comparison to the main plot.

SYMBOL

An object, *character,* figure, or color that is used to represent an abstract idea or concept. Unlike an *emblem,* a symbol may have different meanings in different contexts.

SYNTAX

The way the words in a piece of writing are put together to form lines, phrases, or clauses; the basic structure of a piece of writing.

THEME

A fundamental and universal idea explored in a literary work.

TONE

The author's attitude toward the subject or *characters* of a story or poem or toward the reader.

VOICE

An author's individual way of using language to reflect his or her own personality and attitudes. An author communicates voice through *tone, diction,* and *syntax.*

A Note on Plagiarism

Plagiarism—presenting someone else's work as your own—rears its ugly head in many forms. Many students know that copying text without citing it is unacceptable. But some don't realize that even if you're not quoting directly, but instead are paraphrasing or summarizing, *it is plagiarism* unless you cite the source.

Here are the most common forms of plagiarism:

- Using an author's phrases, sentences, or paragraphs without citing the source
- Paraphrasing an author's ideas without citing the source
- Passing off another student's work as your own

How do you steer clear of plagiarism? You should *always* acknowledge all words and ideas that aren't your own by using quotation marks around verbatim text or citations like footnotes and endnotes to note another writer's ideas. For more information on how to give credit when credit is due, ask your teacher for guidance or visit www.sparknotes.com.

REVIEW & RESOURCES

QUIZ

1. What is the source of the fortune that Judge Thatcher is keeping in trust for Huck?

    A. Buried treasure
    B. Huck's father's life insurance policy
    C. A robber's stash that Huck and Tom found in a cave
    D. An inheritance from Huck's mother

2. At the end of the novel, which character informs the others that Jim is actually a free man?

    A. Aunt Polly
    B. Tom
    C. Huck
    D. Sid

3. Which of the following symbolizes bad luck to Huck and Jim?

    A. A shed snakeskin
    B. Jim's hairy chest
    C. Rain
    D. The wrecked steamboat

4. Which Wilks sister is initially suspicious of Huck?

    A. Mary Jane
    B. Susan
    C. Joanna
    D. Sophia

5. How does Huck know that Pap has returned to St. Petersburg?

   A. Tom tells him.
   B. Pap visits Judge Thatcher to demand Huck's money.
   C. The authorities determine that the corpse found in the river is not Pap.
   D. He sees Pap's boot print in the snow.

6. What is the name of the wrecked steamboat on which Huck and Jim encounter the robbers?

   A. The *Royal Nonesuch*
   B. The *Walter Scott*
   C. The *Mississippi Queen*
   D. The *New Orleans*

7. What is Jim's initial destination when he and Huck start downriver?

   A. New Orleans
   B. An Arkansas plantation
   C. St. Louis
   D. The Ohio River

8. Where does Huck hide the Wilks family gold?

   A. In Peter Wilks's coffin
   B. In the basement
   C. In a mattress
   D. In an old cabin in the woods

9. Down which river do Huck and Jim travel?

   A. The Missouri
   B. The Mississippi
   C. The Ohio
   D. The Chattahoochee

10. What event sets off the final gunfight between the Shepherdsons and the Grangerfords?

    A. The death of Harney Shepherdson
    B. The theft of the Grangerfords' cattle
    C. Sophia Grangerford's elopement with a Shepherdson
    D. An insult to Colonel Grangerford

11. How do Huck and Jim initially acquire the raft?

    A. They steal it.
    B. They build it.
    C. They buy it from a slave trader.
    D. They find it during a flood.

12. What does the "witch pie" that Huck and Tom bake for Jim contain?

    A. A rope ladder
    B. A pen made from a brass candlestick
    C. An old shirt and a spoon
    D. A dead snake

13. How do the duke and the dauphin dress Jim so that he can stay on the raft without being tied up?

    A. As a young girl
    B. As a sick Arab
    C. As a camel
    D. As a Shakespearean actor

14. What is the name of the town where Huck, Jim, and Tom live at the novel's opening?

    A. Cairo
    B. St. Louis
    C. Pikesville
    D. St. Petersburg

REVIEW & RESOURCES

15. Why does Jim run away from Miss Watson's?

    A.   She treats him poorly.
    B.   She is planning to sell him, which would separate him from his family.
    C.   He wants to see relatives in New Orleans.
    D.   He wants to help Huck escape his father.

16. What charm does Jim wear around his neck that he says cures sickness?

    A.   A silver key
    B.   A five-cent piece
    C.   A snake tooth
    D.   A rabbit's foot

17. Which of the following is the primary influence on Tom Sawyer?

    A.   His Aunt Polly
    B.   Sunday school
    C.   Adventure novels
    D.   Abolitionist speeches

18. "Temperance" refers to the movement designed to abolish which of the following?

    A.   Drinking alcohol
    B.   Slavery
    C.   School segregation
    D.   Income taxes

19. What kind of animal does Huck kill as part of the plot to fake his own death?

    A.   A dog
    B.   A deer
    C.   A fish
    D.   A pig

20. Who finally tells Huck that Pap is dead?

    A.   Tom

    B.   Aunt Polly

    C.   Jim

    D.   Sally Phelps

21. Which of the following characters gets shot in Jim's final "escape"?

    A.   Huck

    B.   Tom

    C.   Jim

    D.   All of the above

22. Where does Huck go after Sherburn disperses the lynch mob?

    A.   To the police

    B.   To the raft

    C.   To the circus

    D.   To the theater

23. What is Mark Twain's real name?

    A.   William Jennings Bryan

    B.   Henry Williams Norris

    C.   William Dean Howells

    D.   Samuel Clemens

24. How does Tom travel to the Phelps farm?

    A.   By steamboat

    B.   By horse-cart

    C.   By foot

    D.   By train

25. Where does Huck intend to go at the novel's end?

    A.   St. Petersburg
    B.   The West
    C.   New York City
    D.   The Phelps farm

Suggestions for Further Reading

BUDD, LOUIS J., ed. *New Essays on* THE ADVENTURES OF HUCKLEBERRY FINN. Cambridge: Cambridge University Press, 1985.

CHADWICK-JOSHUA, JOCELYN. *The Jim Dilemma: Reading Race in* HUCKLEBERRY FINN. Jackson, MS: University Press of Mississippi, 1998.

DE KOSTER, KATIE, ed. *Readings on* THE ADVENTURES OF HUCKLEBERRY FINN. San Diego: Greenhaven Press, 1998.

DOYNO, VICTOR A. *Writing* HUCK FINN: *Mark Twain's Creative Process*. Philadelphia: University of Pennsylvania Press, 1992.

FISHKIN, SHELLEY FISHER. *Was Huck Black?: Mark Twain and African-American Voices*. New York: Oxford University Press, 1994.

HOFFMAN, ANDREW JAY. *Twain's Heroes, Twain's Worlds*. Philadelphia: University of Pennsylvania Press, 1988.

PIZER, DONALD, ed. *The Cambridge Companion to American Realism and Naturalism: Howells to London*. Cambridge: Cambridge University Press, 1995.

POWERS, RON. *Mark Twain: A Life*. New York: Free Press, 2005.

TWAIN, MARK. *The Adventures of Tom Sawyer*. New York: Penguin Classics, 1986.

———. *Life on the Mississippi*. New York: Penguin Classics, 1986.

WIECK, CARL F. *Refiguring* HUCKLEBERRY FINN. Athens, GA: University of Georgia Press, 2000.